TALKING ABOUT ALDO

JIM DINE
MARCO LIVINGSTONE

TALKING ABOUT ALDO

ENITHARMON EDITIONS

First published in 2008 by
Enitharmon Editions
26B Caversham Road
London NW5 2DU

www.enitharmon.co.uk

Introduction © Marco Livingstone 2008
Interview © Jim Dine and Marco Livingstone 2008
Images © Jim Dine 2008

ISBN: 978-1-904634-68-3 (de luxe)
ISBN: 978-1-904634-69-0 (regular)

ACKNOWLEDGEMENTS

Enitharmon Editions would like to express thanks to
the following for their help in preparing the visual material
for publication: Julia Braun and Elisa Badii at Steidl;
Richard Solomon and Judy Tobar at Pace Prints, Inc.;
Alan Cristea, David Cleaton-Roberts
and Camilla Robinson at Alan Cristea Gallery.

The prints made by Jim Dine with Aldo Crommelynck
have been published variously by Atelier Crommelynck, Paris
and by Pace Editions, New York, in the latter case distributed
or co-published for Europe by Waddington Graphics, London
and later by Alan Cristea Gallery, London.

CONTENTS

PARIS SMILES: THE MEETING OF TWO MASTERS

Marco Livingstone

7

TALKING ABOUT ALDO, PART 1

11

TALKING ABOUT ALDO, PART 2

57

LIST OF ILLUSTRATIONS

71

LIST OF PRINTS MADE BY JIM DINE
WITH ALDO CROMMELYNCK

73

COLOPHON

76

In memory of Pep Crommelynck

Jim Dine with Aldo Crommelynck in the courtyard of Atelier Crommelynck
at 172 rue de Grenelle in the early 1980s

PARIS SMILES: THE MEETING OF TWO MASTERS

Even in the context of the huge resurgence of printmaking since the 1960s, the 121 prints made by the American artist Jim Dine (born 1935) in collaboration with the French master printer Aldo Crommelynck (born 1931) between 1976 and 1997 form one of the most impressive and sustained investigations into the possibilities of intaglio printmaking since the death of Picasso in 1973. Crommelynck, by common consent one of the outstanding intaglio printers of the 20th century, in fact attracted Picasso's attention after beginning work as an apprentice to Roger Lacourière in 1947; he soon became Picasso's favourite printer, responsible, for example, for the celebrated *347 Gravures* in 1968. Later he printed, too, for such eminent Ecole de Paris artists as Braque, Matisse, Miró, Rouault, Masson, Léger and Giacometti. By the time he first invited Dine into his workshop, Crommelynck had also worked with some of the leading artists of the post-Picasso generation, including Richard Hamilton and David Hockney. During the 1970s and 1980s he printed with Jasper Johns, Avigdor Arikha, R. B. Kitaj, Alex Katz, Howard Hodgkin and David Salle, among others.

Meticulous and systematic, immensely creative and sensitive to the distinct needs of each artist, Crommelynck was prepared for anything, including the often highly unconventional, at times even wild, ways of Dine, who was prepared to use whatever methods or implements would give him the most efficient, powerful and intense results, including even power tools intended for home carpentry. By the mid-1970s Dine had already produced an immense and internationally admired body of graphic work encompassing etching, drypoint, lithography, screenprinting and woodcut. Having always enjoyed the challenge of working with different printers and workshops, from the most sophisticated to the most primitive, Dine, too, was ready to rise to the challenge of creating some of his own most ambitious etchings in association with the man with whom Picasso had produced so many of his late masterpieces. Dine's first set of four prints with Aldo were a kind of tribute to him and his neighbourhood, in that they represented the Eiffel Tower as seen from just outside the premises that Crommelynck had established in 1969 on the rue de Grenelle in the seventh arrondissement.

Initially politely respectful of each other, Dine and Crommelynck soon found a deep and lifelong friendship blossoming, and through Aldo Jim began to deepen his knowledge and appreciation of French life and culture. Never one to miss an opportunity to produce more creative work or to extend the possibilities of his language in any chosen medium, Dine began to pass through Paris with increasing frequency, taking advantage as often as he could of the opportunities to work in the Atelier Crommelynck. Probably the single most astonishing product of these sometimes brief and impromptu visits were the 25 variations produced between 1978 and 1981 of a large-scale portrait of his first wife, Nancy, under the collective title *Nancy Outside in July*. This series – a virtuoso performance that explores numerous possibilities of intaglio printmaking and even invents new ones – is reason enough in itself to celebrate the meeting between the two men, each a master in his own field.

The prints made by Dine with Crommelynck encompass a wide range of his signature motifs, including not only the portraits of Nancy but also hearts, robes, tools, plants and flowers, skulls, the Venus de Milo, owls and ravens – not forgetting, of course, the wrought-iron gate outside the Crommelynck workshop, which became a favourite motif also in works made in other mediums, including woodcuts, drawings, paintings and sculptures. To see all this work together, as was finally possible through the artist's generosity in making a gift of all these prints to the Bibliothèque Nationale in Paris in 2006, is an exhilarating experience. This sizeable slice alone of Dine's immense and dazzling graphic production, now well on the way to a thousand separate sheets, provides an immensely stimulating object lesson in the continuing possibilities of intaglio methods deeply rooted in tradition but as alive and as challenging as ever.

Dine's vivid, candid and detailed reminiscences about his friendship and working relationship with Crommelynck over a period now of more than 30 years are full of affection, humour and layer upon layer of information. During conversations conducted in Paris and London, the artist charts the extent to which his experience of working with a man who was not only a great printer, but also a skilled draughtsman, an aesthete, dandy and bon viveur, coloured and enriched his experience of France on every level, from an appreciation of its art and culture, its city life and countryside, to its food and its specialist shops – including those in which to find the best tools or musical instruments. Dine's ruminations take some unexpected but illuminating detours, even into the making of bespoke bicycles, that prove deeply revealing of the specific nature of his love for France and of his many debts to an esteemed colleague, fellow traveller and much loved friend.

MARCO LIVINGSTONE

JIM DINE & MARCO LIVINGSTONE
TALKING ABOUT ALDO

PART 1: PARIS, 15 JANUARY 2006

MARCO LIVINGSTONE: How did you and Aldo first meet?

JIM DINE: Paul Cornwall-Jones told me that Richard Hamilton had found a printer here, and that I should go try him. That he was Picasso's printer, blah blah blah. That's either how it happened, or Richard told me about Aldo.

ML: Aldo couldn't remember, and then at the very end of the interview he suddenly thought that maybe it was Richard, who had just come to work on that *Homage to Picasso* portfolio.

JD: My *Homage to Picasso* piece was not done here, it was done with a lithographer in Berlin.

ML: You had been etching in London before then.

JD: With Maurice Payne.

ML: So why would Paul Cornwall-Jones have been recommending another printer?

JD: Well, in the first place because Aldo had the reputation as the greatest in the world, that was probably why, through his work with Picasso. And Paul was always finding situations that were interesting for us to go to.

ML: How much did you know about Aldo's work with other artists?

JD: I knew nothing.

ML: You hadn't seen any of the prints he had made with other people?

JD: I'm sure I had, but I didn't know that he had printed them. I knew the Braques, I knew the late Matisses and I knew the Picassos, but I had no idea that he had printed them. I think I was probably still thinking [they had been printed by Roger] Lacourière.

ML: How old is Aldo now?

JD: I think he is 74 or just turned 75.

ML: So when he worked with Matisse, he was barely 20.

JD: Oh, yeah, probably in his late teens. His father suggested that he apprentice himself to Lacourière when he was 17. Eventually he went to work for Picasso exclusively for a while. Every morning he would meet Jacqueline Picasso on the metro, they would both be coming to Picasso's. That was, I think, '52, and I think he was 22. So he is four or five years older than me.

ML: Were you fired up by the knowledge that as a very young man Aldo had worked with Picasso and Matisse?

JD: It was just part of the basic mythology. You have to understand that when I got here [to Paris], I wasn't even clear as to why I was here. What was I going to do? I go to the rue de Grenelle and I meet this guy who I could hardly see, not just because he was so slim but because he is so retiring and shy, very formal. I had to carry the whole thing: 'What are we going to do? What's the deal?' He talked about techniques, all of which I knew about except

Facing page: detail from *Technicolor II*, 1996 (see page 55)

I put questions to him about certain things I wanted to do. He said, 'We could do it this way.' He was a big advocate always of sugar lift, and I always felt it just took too long and it was not in my bag of tricks. But I did use it over the years with him, finally, and it always worked perfectly. But you have to leave too much to the printer, and in those days I wasn't willing to give up much. It was always such a secretive place. He had phones, buzzer systems. Sometimes [Aldo's wife] Pep would come silently down, come in, say something to Aldo and he would give her something – I always presumed they were exchanging cash – and I would see her walk off with a market bag. I'd see her come back, but she'd never stop back in. I guess he introduced her to me once, but I was certainly never invited upstairs. Whereas I think Richard [Hamilton] was immediately invited upstairs; I think Richard even stayed there. I was never invited to stay there, which I would never have done, anyway. I don't like those situations.

ML: But you became great friends later, so what was the process?

JD: I am going to give you the process. So the first time I go there, I figured I'd do something about Paris. The first things I made with Aldo were the etchings about the Eiffel Tower. Firstly, he lived near it, and he was very much of his *quartier*, always talking about the Avenue Bosquet, the rue Cler, La Motte Picquet, the Ecole Militaire, la Tour Eiffel and the Champs de Mars. It was all in his neighbourhood, and he was a great fan of the neighbourhood.

ML: And at that time he hadn't been there that many years. He moved there in 1966 or 1968?

JD: I don't know when the house was finished. In fact, it has never been finished. Even in the studio there were light bulbs coming out of the walls with just bare wire. But I think I got there when it had just been done, in the last five or six years. It looked like it. We started to work. I think it was the summertime. But I would never see him socially, and I never had lunch with him. I would come, leave for lunch and go back in the afternoon to see the proofs.

ML: How good was his English then?

JD: Just like now.

ML: So you had no trouble communicating with him?

JD: Not really, no. As a boy he was sent with his cousin Florent to England. His father was a famous playwright between the wars in Paris, a Belgian but living in Paris. He knew everybody, including Picasso. He knew a lot of British painters and bohemians and writers. He sent him to Finch's pub on the Fulham Road, where I used to go when I first came to England. You could see all these old drunks there and young women. It was like a bohemian pick-up place and like a club house in a certain way. He and Florent were, I guess, 15 or 16. It helped his English. He speaks with an English accent rather than an American one. And, of course, his English improved when he [later] went to America. When I have been away, he sometimes can't think of the words, but it comes back to him once we spend some nights with him.

ML: And when you first came to work with Aldo, he was in partnership with...

JD: ...his brother Piero. It was the Atelier Crommelynck, and I was immediately introduced to the brother. For almost 15 years, the door was open, there was a common office and you came into the studio. Piero was in the office at times. He was very much a poseur, 'so tired' and 'so stressed', but he did nothing.

He clearly did nothing. Except he doled out the money. When I wanted money – you see, they were publishers, too. He said, 'Will Paul [Cornwall-Jones] publish this, or will I?' And I said, since it was just the time I was leaving Paul, 'Why don't you publish it?' That way he paid the production, and they sold it. People came to the Crommelyncks and they would buy prints. Alan Cristea would come from Marlborough, all sorts of dealers would come, and private people. I sent lots of private Americans there to buy.

ML: And who handled that, Piero?

JD: Piero. The business side was Piero. Like when I needed cash, I thought I would always have to have it remitted back to my account, but very quickly I realised that I had a little bank here, because he was selling my prints. So I'd say, could I have a hundred Francs or a thousand Francs, whatever it is. Piero would go into the acid room, the biting room where the aquatint box was…

ML: Where they were printing off the notes, too.

JD: [Laughs.] No! They must have built a safe into the wall. I never saw. He would go in there. Every time it was the same thing, and I'm not supposed to notice this, you know? It was so Old World. He'd go in there and come back always with all these fresh Francs. So maybe he *was* printing them! He'd have them in his pocket and then hand them to me surreptitiously. There would only be three of us there: me, Aldo and Piero. And he'd hand them to me and that would be that. Then I wouldn't see Piero much. He'd come in and shake my hand. I had about four or five meals at his house in all those years. He had this very spooky wife. I had gotten a commission once to make a portrait of a woman who collected my drawings, an Italian woman who was the heiress to Martini & Rossi and lived in Torino or Milano or something. Very beautiful, elegant woman. And she told me, because she had been a great friend of Marino Marini's, that Piero had acquired his collection of Picassos by giving the wife in trade. That Marino told her that. She loved this story and told me this. It never occurred to me, but I do remember going to his apartment before, and in the apartment were like thirty pastel portraits of Piero and pictures of the child and the wife.

ML: Where has all that gone?

JD: It must be in Piero's apartment. He died three or four years ago. There was an obituary on the front page of *Le Monde*, and Jean-Luc Monterosso called me and said, 'I'm really sorry to hear about your friend.' I said, 'That wasn't my friend, that was my enemy. That's the brother.' Monterosso and Aldo get on very well. But it shows you the quality of Piero's lying all these years, and Aldo's retiring nature, that everybody thought Piero was the printer for Picasso. Everyone thought Piero did everything, that Piero was the important one. And he fucked Aldo out of his birthright in a certain way. First of all, he took all of Aldo's money. They had been partners in this other business of lawn furniture. When Picasso died and the print market was going to shit for some reason at that point, Aldo said, 'Listen. We need something else. We've got a big house here, we've got overheads, you've got a kid.' Aldo was a great anglophile, he had English girlfriends and English friends, and contacted somebody and got the franchise for the teak lawn furniture that you see everywhere now, from the Duke of Devonshire, Chatsworth. They had a shop over by the Invalides, rather grand. They imported Italian beach umbrellas, because Piero went to Italy, and they had this very austere, Aldo-like furniture. And it was a success. I can't remember the name of it; they've moved since, to right here on the rue du Bac. That was the beginning of the end. Piero had everything in his wife's name, and Aldo was never able to get the business from him. When they split, he just took that, and Aldo didn't push it. It was very tragic, the whole thing.

ML: I was going to ask how you came to work together, but you've already explained that you came specifically to Paris to meet him with the intention of working with him.

JD: Yes, and that's how I heard about him.

ML: You had been working in various printmaking mediums since the early 1960s, primarily lithography and etching but also screenprinting.

JD: And woodcuts...

ML: Your first etchings, a series of five representing men's neckties, were made in 1961, though lithography predominated during that decade. During the early 1970s you moved from intaglio methods to lithography as the opportunities arose. With Petersburg Press in London you had produced some of your most intense and intimate intaglio work, such as the *Photographs and Etchings* portfolio with Lee Friedlander in 1969, the *Four Kinds of Pubic Hair* etchings of 1971, the six states of *Five Paintbrushes* in 1972, the two states of *Braid* in 1972 and 1973 and – most memorably – the set of 30 drypoints called *Thirty Bones of My Body* in 1972. Would you say that you were more in thrall to etching and drypoint at that time than to lithography, and did you for that reason start looking for other master printers specialising in these processes, so that you could further extend your investigations of them?

JD: I almost by that point had turned my back on lithography. To me it was so flat, it felt flat, and etching was giving me such an electric line. Hard-ground etching was also, with the way I was working, very conducive to the image I was making: the pubic hair, paint brushes, all that kind of stuff, hair and bristles. It just felt good, and I was not looking for other printers. I would always be interested to work in a different shop. Every time I've done it, I've learned something different. And with Aldo, while I was printing these things – they weren't printed just by Maurice Payne, a lot of them were printed by Winston Roeth and Alan Uglow, who were printers Paul had in New York. So I might proof the plates with Maurice and then take them to New York and edition them there, or just work with them directly. I forget who did what; it's all recorded in the catalogue raisonné. But with Aldo, here's what I was getting. [Allen] Ginsberg said once that he had this direct link to Walt Whitman, because he had had sex with the last lover. So this is what it was like with Aldo and Picasso and me. I had this link to this mythic figure.

ML: You never met Picasso?

JD: No, never. Nor would I want do. What would you say, 'Gee, I love your work'? Did Hockney meet him?

ML: No, Hockney didn't meet him, and he regrets that he didn't.

JD: I don't regret it at all. It would have just been a pissing match, a macho thing.

ML: It's often best not to meet your heroes, anyway, because if you don't like them as people, or if there was a competitiveness...

JD: Absolutely. Something would have happened. It would have been 'old bull', 'young bull' kind of thing. I know it. I asked Aldo, 'How did Picasso die?' He said, 'Well, he caught a cold and he didn't come one day into work, so they sent for the doctor, or they said "Don't come up, we'll get the plates", and he just went to bed and died.' Aldo is full of stories about Picasso and those years on the Riviera. It seemed Aldo was quite a playboy, in a way, down there in the sixties. He was a pilot, and he had girlfriends and stuff.

ML: There are a number of references to French literature in your work of the late 1960s and early 1970s, notably in the book *The Poet Assassinated* (1968), in the eight etched portraits of Rimbaud in 1972–3 and in the two editions of the four *Flaubert Favorites* lithographs in 1972. In 1971 you had also made some collage paintings and related prints dedicated to the French Dadaist Francis Picabia. Was there a particular love affair with 19th-century French culture and the origins of modernism that also was drawing you to Paris and to French traditions?

JD: Aldo drew me to Paris, but being in Paris awakened in me the collective memory of French culture, and I wanted to be a part of it and be a part of the light. I was experiencing the same light that Pissarro had seen. I still feel that, but I'm an old guy now and I am much more realistic. I was very romantic about France then. I never spoke French. I never wanted to even make an effort, and it wasn't my aptitude, anyway. It was a pleasure not to speak French, it was a pleasure to be quiet and look. That's what I did the whole time. I looked, and I walked on the boulevards, and Aldo and I had long conversations about what hardware store to go to, where do you buy this, about bike makers. 'What brand is your bike, Aldo?' He told me about a man called René Herse in the suburbs in Pontoise, and he said, 'This man will make you a bike.'

And I said, 'OK, I want one of those, Let's go out there.' So he took me out there. It was a great experience. The man was one of the last great artisans for cycles. His daughter, who worked there, had been a tandem champion, and the other person who worked there was a famous mechanic who was the daughter's lover. It was a whole life of amateur cycling. It had started before the war and continued into the war and after the war, and it was just petering out as he was getting old into the seventies. So I said, 'I'd like a touring bike.' It took him, I think, two years to make, and it cost me $500, or $700 maybe, even. A bike like that is sold on eBay for maybe $10,000 or $12,000 now. I still have mine, it's in the basement of my house at Jane Street in New York. I'm about to have it restored by a very good mechanic. I have another one by Herse hanging up here that I use a lot, but that wasn't made for me. It was a demo and I bought it, because it fit. I was interested in this artisan culture in France, and Aldo was, too.

ML: The works relating to France that I was asking you about preceded your first meeting with Aldo by several years. *The Poet Assassinated* was 1968.

JD: I was interested in France, of course. The Rimbaud images began around the time of those visits to Aldo. I found on the quais a magazine called *Historia* that had Rimbaud's portrait on the cover.

ML: But those prints were not made with Aldo...

JD: Not at all. They were made before, and then while I was working with him.

ML: For an American artist of your generation, given the previous generation's long process of detaching themselves from France – from the Abstract Expressionists onwards – for you, ten years into your career, to go back to France was quite unusual, I would think.

JD: Very.

ML: It was unusual that you were comfortable about reconnecting with that tradition.

JD: Not only comfortable. It thrilled me. It was like having a girlfriend. In fact I had a French girlfriend in those years, too. That was thrilling, too! To know a French woman.

ML: In your preface to the *Nancy Outside in July* book published by ULAE in 1983 on the occasion of your exhibition of those prints at the Art Institute of Chicago, you paid respectful tribute to Aldo as your 'collaborator', saying bluntly that 'He is so much greater than any other in the world that to call him Printer is all that is necessary.' That is an amazing accolade! Can you expand on what makes him the greatest printer with whom you have worked?

JD: [Long pause.] No, I'm going to be frank about it. I'm the greatest printer. I merely used his facilities, as it were. He was the channel for this. He was particular. He demanded an even edition. He printed in a way that the image was foremost. You weren't even aware of the paper. They had so much pressure. It was like going to a great laundry, and your shirts looked like new. That's the way he printed. He rarely gave me anything but the facilities to use to go ahead. *Nancy Outside in July* was the first time I really expanded my technical skills. Not only technical skills, but my interest in how you could make prints and keep on printing through. It's just like an eating and shitting kind of thing, a whole digestive tract history of intaglio printing. He did great aquatints, spit-bite, showed me how to use it. But he's intimidating, too. He restrained me, so that a lot of the expressive things in my prints came after Aldo, or when I was working with other printers, or in my own studio, where I could throw acid around. Hamilton always laughs at the story about one day I showed up at Aldo's, when I wasn't supposed to come. Aldo was very discreet and scrupulous. He would not book you in if another artist was there. I appreciated that, I can't stand it if there are other artists. But one day I showed up to say hi, I think on the spur of the moment. I think Nancy was with me, and I think we'd stopped over in England and I said, 'Let's go say hello to Aldo and Pep'. This was in the early '80s. And Hamilton was there working. Aldo sort of gave me the idea that I could work. He said, 'Do you want to do anything?' 'Yeah', I said. I made a three-panelled work, *Desire in Primary Colors* [1982]. I said, 'Give me some old plates.' I think I took some of the *Nancy* plates, and I took his grinder and just started. I don't know what I was thinking. There was Hamilton, in the same room, sitting at the same table with me. I must say, he's a good sport, because he laughed about it later. I shot metal filings over his prints and everything else. I just came in like a cyclone. And Aldo just stayed back, cowering. He didn't know what to do. He understood Richard's complete opposite-side-of-the-coin, surgical, behaviour. He just never saw anything like it, and he didn't know what was going to happen. But Richard just laughed. He thought it was a riot.

ML: I got this story from Aldo, too, slightly differently!

JD: Oh, really! What did he say?

ML: He said that you had arrived in Paris and had rung him up to say, 'I'd like to come in and work.' And he said, 'Oh, it's a bit difficult, because Richard's here', but you went in anyway. He did tell me about the grinding and the bits of metal shooting up in the air.

JD: I'm a lot more sensitive now than I was then! [Laughs.]

ML: One of the texts that you wrote for our *Alchemy of Images* monograph [1998], 'Me and Aldo', opens with the remarks: 'I began etching with Aldo Crommelynck in 1973 just after Picasso had died, thus freeing Aldo to work with us mortals.' Was it really that early? Because the Eiffel Tower prints are listed in the catalogue raisonné as 1976.

JD: No. That's wrong. Maybe they weren't released until 1976.

ML: That's part of the problem I've had in trying to make sense of all this, because the dates in the catalogue raisonné, of course, are usually the dates of publication. And what the entries don't tell you is when the plates were made.

JD: So when did Picasso die?

ML: 1973 [8 April].

JD: So I must have come to work here in '74.

ML: But they are all dated 1976 in the catalogue raisonné. Do you remember if there was a long gap between you working on the plates and them actually being published?

JD: I have no idea.

ML: And you didn't come first just to meet Aldo, and not do any work, and then return a couple of years later to make those first etchings with him? That three-year difference perplexed me.

JD: I don't recall. I think I came, met him, and then we started to work. I ordered the plate sizes. But it does make sense that it was after the break with Paul Cornwall-Jones, because Aldo published that stuff. And at the time I was with [Ileanna] Sonnabend, and she wasn't interested in prints. I left Petersburg Press by '74, '75. By that time we were in litigation, because my lawyer certainly knew Paul Cornwall-Jones well. And it suddenly occurred to him to say to me, 'This isn't fair what's going on. You know that he's doubling production costs and taking it out first, and that's your money.' At the same time there was a guy called David Begelman in Hollywood who was caught doing the same thing, and actors blew the whistle on him. Paul did that, too. Every time he sent a car to Heathrow to pick me up, I thought it was a pleasure. I thought he was being nice, but it was a double cost for the car for me. Every tuna fish sandwich that I thought he gave me was charged to me. And Stuart said, 'He just can't do this.' I didn't have enough smarts at the time to say, 'Look, I don't care. What I really want to do is to keep working with Paul, because he's a genius, and he and I make a lot of good work together and inspire each other.' Which I didn't do. He literally turned me against Paul, and Paul was so fucked up that he went along with it and got a lawyer, too, who knew my lawyer. We spent a lot of money until finally we came to an agreement, we split everything and went our ways.

ML: You split everything in terms of getting half the editions back.

JD: I got half the editions back, exactly. I don't think I got any cash. Then we went on our way, and I never worked with Paul again and I didn't speak to him again for another 25 years. I never ran into him, even. And he got out of the print business. And it was too bad. Maybe it was just for that moment, anyway, but the combination we had with Hamilton, me and David [Hockney], and at one time Eduardo [Paolozzi]…

ML: He did a lot of very imaginative and inventive projects, including Patrick Caulfield's illustrations to Laforgue, Hockney's *Grimms' Fairy Tales*...

JD: Oh, yeah. Incredible.

ML: More than any other print publisher in England before or since.

JD: Absolutely. He really revitalised and raised the level, even more than Tanya Grossman. This guy walked the walk. He really came through. For many years I missed his friendship.

ML: He fell out with most of the artists eventually, because of money.

JD: Yes, because of money. He couldn't help himself. There was no reason to cheat us. He was making money, and we were. So, anyway, about '74 or '75 we were breaking up. I remember Paul being with me in Bordeaux, when I had a show at the Entrepôt down there. That was '75. He came with me, he was on the train with me, but that was about the end. So about that time I was going to Aldo, and about that time I was leaving Sonnabend. In 1976 I went to Pace [in New York]. That's when I started to make prints heavily with Pace Editions. I would still do a little bit with Tanya Grossman, but not much; she was dying. So I preferred working with Dick Solomon [at Pace Editions], and Dick liked Aldo, and he said, 'Publish what you want to publish and we'll sell it.' It all worked out OK.

ML: It may be that your first contact with Aldo may have been as late as 1975, and you remembered it as 1973 because you felt Picasso's shadow still on you.

JD: Maybe. When did Richard [Hamilton] go?

ML: Richard went in 1973, immediately after Picasso died.

JD: So I probably went in 1975. That sounds likely to me. If those came out in '76, we wouldn't have sat on them for three years.

ML: The first prints you made with Aldo in 1976 were the four featuring the Eiffel Tower, the quintessential – almost, one might say, impossibly corny – Parisian monument, which happens to loom over that stretch of the rue de Grenelle where Aldo lived and ran his studio. Did the subject choose you, or impose itself on you, as the obvious choice with which to begin your collaboration?

JD: That was when I was in love with Paris. It chose me, yes, exactly. I was positively hot for Paris.

ML: It's not as though anyone could have predicted from your earlier work that you would have chosen such an architectural subject.

JD: The Eiffel Tower, yeah. I guess I could have chosen a croissant or something like that, who knows? But I thought this was so...

ML: Or French shoes!

JD: Yes, exactly.

ML: The Eiffel Tower is, of course, one of the must-see destinations of a tourist newly arrived in Paris for the first time. You had been to Paris only briefly on a couple of occasions before this, hadn't you, in 1968 and 1970?

JD: I was here in '68 at the time of the 'événements de Mai', because I remember it. I was right in the middle of it, in the Latin Quarter. I was here to make prints with Déjoubert and another guy, an etcher, whom Aldo knew well. Paul [Cornwall-Jones] and I were doing

Dorian Gray. So that's why I was here. It was the first time I came. No, it was the second time I came. I'd been the winter before to meet Déjoubert. There were two reasons I hadn't come over to Paris immediately were (one), I was afraid of the French, because of the American hang-up about 'Let's get away from French culture, we're American cowboys'. The other was I was afraid of flying, so I didn't move so easily. Then I realised you could take the boat train from Victoria Station, so with great trepidation I got on the train one night, sharing the compartment with a guy. I didn't know anything about purchasing a single compartment. We went to sleep…all night long I was tossing and turning, and when I woke up we had gotten off the ship and back onto the land, and you couldn't see out of the window, there was so much ice and snow. I guess it came into the Gare du Nord. I went from there immediately to Déjoubert's. This was probably January or February of 1968. Paul was already here, maybe doing business with David [Hockney]. Hans-Jörg [Mayer] was also here, me and Paul. I was on the way to Rome, to work on a film, *A Quiet Place in the Country* [1968], [starring] Franco Nero. It was about a painter, and I was painting the paintings. So I got back on the train and took the train to Rome, that day. I didn't stay that day in Paris. I just had lunch with them. It was my first taste of Paris. It was exactly the way I thought it was going to be, too. It was so fabulous. The next time was to come in '68, during the 'événements de Mai'. This time I think it was to work on the etchings. Both lithographs and etchings. There was certainly no mention of Crommelynck. I wasn't aware of his existence. But I certainly felt energised; I loved the place. It took me many years before I went to the Louvre.

ML: You avoided it.

JD: Yes, absolutely. I didn't want any of that rubbing off on me.

ML: But to choose the Eiffel Tower: were you in that sense stating your position as an American confronted at last with an almost mythical Paris that you had known only in photographs, or through art and literature? Were you kind of presenting yourself, in other words, as a tourist by choosing the Eiffel Tower?

JD: It didn't occur to me. I wanted to celebrate myself in Paris. As I said, I was having a mild affair with a French woman, and that was exciting. Wait a minute: Paul knew about it, so I was still [working] with Paul. It was just transitional. These things were probably meant for Paul, and as it changed, Aldo said, 'I'll publish them.' That's what happened. There was a party on the rue de Seine at a friend of David [Hockney's] called Jean Léger. Kasmin was there, David. Jean Léger fixed me up with this girl. She had said, 'I'd like to meet him' or something, I don't know. I am talking about 1973, when we were living in Vermont. David [Hockney] had Tony Richardson's flat, the Balthus flat. Paul made mention of it [the affair] in passing, just so he could let me know that he knew my business. He said, 'How is Nicole?' or something like that. Asshole. So that must have been the transition. So I would say it was '75 when I was working on them. I actually think the drypoint of the Eiffel Tower may even have been proofed in America, or I cut it in America, maybe. [The catalogue raisonné entry indicates that it was printed and published by Crommelynck.] I have some memory that these weren't all just done at the rue de Grenelle.

ML: How accurate is the catalogue raisonné on that type of thing? There's quite a lot of detail in the entries.

JD: I don't know, I haven't looked at it.

ML: It strikes me, though, that the motif of the Eiffel Tower relates to certain shapes you had favoured in earlier years: there is a strong similarity, for instance, with the *Plant Becomes a Fan* series of sculptures as reconfigured in a series of five lithographs in 1974.

JD: Right.

ML: And – if you invert the shape – there is a similarity with the pubic hair pencil drawings on vellum and related etchings of 1970–71.

JD: Exactly. I just saw that!

ML: Were you aware of that at the time?

JD: No.

ML: Might it have been a subliminal connection?

JD: Well, possibly, because as I said, it was a sexy time for me.

ML: Because the tower is also a kind of phallic symbol.

JD: Yes, exactly.

ML: And that again relates to some of your recent sexual imagery. Do you think you might have subconsciously been drawn to the Eiffel Tower as a subject also because of these formal resemblances, as a way of turning an unfamiliar location into artistically familiar territory?

JD: Yeah, I do. But also to celebrate the exuberance I felt here.

ML: To stick with the Eiffel Tower prints for a moment, it is striking that the simplicity of the imagery is complemented by the layering of processes on each: etching, drypoint, lift and soft-ground printed from either four or five separate plates. Were you in these prints consciously exploring the primary range of processes offered at the Atelier Crommelynck?

JD: Probably, because I had never printed with anyone so sophisticated, in terms of layers. He had what turned out to be a very primitive system of registration, where he would drill a hole in the plate and fix the paper with a pin, so that it would get on right and it was always correct. Since then people have always made fun of it. Kurt Zein said he came to see him in the eighties some time to pay homage to the great man, and he said, 'The fucking holes he was drilling in the plate! I never had to do that in my life. I knew how to register by working it out on the press exact.' These were tiny little holes, but there was no reason. He was offering me multicoloured etchings, and I said, 'I want some of that', because at that point I had made black-and-white etchings, period. That's what I thought you did, or you hand-coloured them. I didn't want to take the time to think. But in fact my mind works like that. My mind is a layered mind, with printing: it's so natural for me. To think, in the first place, backwards. Also to think about how to put the colour on, what's going to come. I lay in bed and think about things like that: you know, what's the next state going to be on top? And he afforded that. He would show me examples of things. Also, Aldo showed me some other things that I am still staggered by, and that is how he was trained. Lacourière said to him, 'You have to wipe the plates', and he did all that, but he also had him doing 'estampes', which were essentially forgeries in intaglio of a painting or a drawing.

ML: Reproductions of existing works.

JD: Yes, reproductions.

ML: And they did that a lot.

JD: A lot! And the artists signed them, and they made a lot of money. And they didn't have to do anything, the artists. Picasso or Braque would leave him a painting. So for three years Aldo would sit there and carve it, and make it.

ML: So Aldo would actually make the plate.

JD: Yes. That's how he learned a lot of technique. I've seen one in a woman's apartment, a long time ago, when Pep and Aldo and I were just getting friendly outside of the work. He took me there, and it was a pencil drawing by Picasso with scotch tape holding it together. But none of it was real. It was all Aldo, in intaglio. It was absolutely exceptional. It was like a forgery, that's what I mean. The guy could have made money, I mean literally: he could have made bills. He was that accurate. Lacourière put him in a competition for etching artists, so he decided to do one. He made this little thing, and he won. It's like a still life with lobster and fish, it's absolutely brilliant.

ML: But he wasn't trained as an artist?

JD: No, he was just good with his hands.

ML: When did he discover that he had that facility?

JD: I guess all his life, don't you think? I think he wanted to be an artist, and I think his father said something *haute bourgeoise* like, 'Artists don't make any money, you should have a trade.' So he got him a job at Lacourière. Aldo was so good, and so intelligent and so brilliant with his hands that he moved up the ladder of this corporation quite fast. And then Picasso wanted him every day.

ML: How long did you stay in Paris on that first occasion working with Aldo?

JD: I wouldn't stay for long in those days. I'd get a hotel and stay for four or five days, then go home.

ML: You'd do your work, proof it, then...

JD: Go back to Vermont, or go back to London and see Paul or see friends in London.

ML: The portfolio of 12 soft-ground etchings that you made with Aldo for the publication called *Mabel* in 1977, for which your friend the American poet Robert Creeley wrote an accompanying prose piece, was your first sustained series of prints with Aldo.

JD: You mean *Mabel* came before *Nancy Outside in July*? Yes.

ML: In their exclusive concentration on human heads, viewed frontally and close up, their contours often cropped by the edges of the plate, they bear particular comparison with the sequences of self-portrait etchings you have made at intervals throughout your life, beginning with the nine drypoints made in 1971, which were reworked in 1975 as *The Dartmouth Portraits*, and also with four of the Rimbaud etchings of 1973. How were the female heads of Mabel arrived at? Were they all purely imagined?

JD: Some were from photographs that I found in magazines.

ML: Just anonymous heads?

JD: Yeah.

ML: It didn't matter who they were.

JD: I was going to do a series with Paul on my friends in London. And I had Paul hire a photographer and send this photographer around who took photographs of my friends. One of the people he photographed was [the artist] Sylvia Guirey. She is one of the people in that book. So maybe some of the other women are, too.

ML: So some of them were faces you knew well, but you were working from photographs.

JD: Right, or some of them were just things I created as I went along in the States. I proofed much of it in Putney with Mitchell Friedman.

ML: But you had already worked on the plates with Aldo?

JD: No, not with Aldo. With Mitchell Friedman. [NB The catalogue raisonné indicates only that they were published and printed by Aldo Crommelynck, making no mention of Friedman.] I editioned them with Aldo.

ML: So Aldo wasn't involved in the creation of those plates, just with the editioning.

JD: He might have, some of the later states, maybe. But my memory is that Mitchell and I did it.

ML: They were all done just at the moment that you had begun drawing the human face and body from life again, an extremely intense activity for you at that time that marked a fundamental shift in your art.

JD: Exactly. It was probably started in 1975, because I started to draw the human figure in 1974.

ML: Was that part of the attraction of that project, that it gave you an excuse to…

JD: Yes, yes, to start some figurative work.

ML: The series of large and technically complex etchings on which you begin work in 1978 – *Nancy Outside in July*…

JD: They were begun in 1978?

ML: Well, they were published in 1978, so there was probably a gap.

JD: …of a year, I would say.

ML: They eventually came to a close in 1981 with the twenty-second print of the series. They really are amongst your masterworks as a printmaker, even now, all these years later.

JD: Yes.

ML: On this occasion, did you travel to Paris with such a project specifically in mind, or did it start life fairly straightforwardly as a portrait of your wife which you thought would be a one-off, and then one thing led to another and you ended up with this huge series?

JD: Yes. The latter. It started off as a portrait of Nancy. At the time I was drawing the figure. I was drawing her a lot. It probably started in Aldo's studio, the first sitting, I would imagine.

ML: And you were drawing directly on the plate?

JD: I was drawing either on the plate, or for the first state I was probably drawing a soft-ground to begin with, and then adding.

ML: Would you like to explain how that works, drawing a soft-ground?

JD: Well, for a soft-ground etching the printer puts down the ground, which never hardens; it's a wax ground that would never dry. And on top of that you put a very thin piece of newsprint, for instance. If I then put my thumb on the newsprint, it would probably print, because the newsprint would pick up that soft-ground.

ML: So you are drawing on the paper, and it's like making a drawing.

JD: Yes, and what you can see is, when you pick the paper up and look at the back, it has picked up the wax, thereby exposing the plate, and the plate gets bit that way. That's the black lines. And it's always a quality of pencil or charcoal, rather than a hardground etching line, which is more like wire. So I began this. I just began it. The first year I worked on that plate, we editioned it, and then we went on to another variation. It just took off from there.

ML: So at no point did you think this was going to be a vast series?

JD: Sure I did. By about the seventh or eighth, I didn't know when it was going to end. And the only reason it ended at all was I guess I was tired. I could have kept this open-ended until I left Nancy. As it was, it was a chronicle of her psychological state through those years.

ML: But after the very first one, where you had her sitting there for you, she was never there again for those later prints?

JD: From time to time I would check with her. I checked what I was doing. She would either come to the studio, or we would have a plate at home in Vermont, and I'd bring it back. Aldo, with this project, became a facilitator. He had nothing more to do with the etching. I was running with the ball, as it were. He was left at the goal line, waiting to see what would happen. The brothers were getting excited to sell these things. They were selling them, and Dick Solomon sold them at Pace.

ML: They were all in different edition sizes, weren't they?

JD: Yeah.

ML: How did you decide how many to print of any particular one. If they weren't published as a portfolio...

JD: One was sold as a portfolio, but even I didn't have the complete portfolio, for the donation I have just made to the Bibliothèque Nationale in Paris, I had a state of the last one. It was a mission I was on, I couldn't stop. The things I could do with printing. Aldo was excited, too. That's the point. Remember I said that we never went upstairs, we never had lunch? At some moment he said, 'Would you like to have lunch?' I remember once I came to work on something. The plane got in late at night. I flew into Paris in the summer time, I came right here and we worked at night, really at night, and then I had to take a taxi, I think to an airport to fly somewhere else, maybe to London. I remember he gave me a bottle of beer from upstairs. He was so accommodating, but he never wanted to interfere or impose himself on something. But we were talking by then, and it was interesting. I mean, we were talking about other things. I'd say, 'Where do you get these drills?' 'Where do you buy your paper?' Then he just invited me upstairs once. Pep was very sweet. But it wasn't until we got into *Nancy Outside in July* and Nancy was here that all four of us would go out to lunch, or I would have lunch with the two of them, and by that time they were getting used to American artists, too. I think Johns had been here for the Beckett thing [*Foirades and Fizzles*, 1976], Hockney had been here: sociable people who they wanted to entertain. Richard was here. So it was great. There were times when I ate two meals a day there every day. 'Of course you will come back for dinner.'

ML: In the third of the *Nancy Outside in July* series, one of the five published in 1978, you added marks produced with electric tools to the more traditionally made marks that characterised the first two prints. Did Aldo take those methods in his stride, or was he a little shocked by them?

JD: I had discovered the use of various electric tools when I was artist-in-residence at Dartmouth College in '73, I think, or '72. That's when I met Mitchell Friedman: he was given to me as an assistant. I'd ask him questions: 'Can't we do something faster? Can't we get an electric tool?' And he said, 'I'll talk to some guys in the sculpture department.' Anyway, he produced something called the die-grinder, which you could erase with. Then you had to use a lot of hand-power to polish it up, but you could keep the line. Then I bought a Dremel in New York. I realised this thing existed, I forget how I got to know about it.

ML: You started looking for tools that were meant for other things.

JD: It's a rotary drill. A Dremel was a hobbyist's tool. I started there, and I realised I could carve copper plates with the Dremel, and it would be like an engraving, not a drypoint. Because a drypoint raises the burr and you print the ink off the burr. But a Dremel is so fast and sharp, it engraves like acid does, or like engraving tools such as a burin. So I started looking for the equivalent in Paris. The Dremel wasn't here yet, quite. The Bon Marché had a hardware department, and the BHV still has a great hardware department, and there I found tools that approximated the Dremel: vibrating needles for hobbyists, or for people marking their own tools. And I also found the things you attached to drills made by a German company called Wolf. They were like sanding discs and sanding brushes, and wire brushes, all kinds of stuff like that. I found them all here first, before I found them in America.

ML: How would you discover then what they were capable of doing? Would you try them out on a test plate, or would you use them actually on the etchings that you were working on?

JD: Always on the etching. I figured that was grist for my mill. I'm going to get some mark. Sometimes it's too black, and then I also found pomades that you could use – a jeweller's polishing thing – and you could put that on the drill, and I'd polish. Aldo was used to sitting there with a knife and scraper, carefully.

ML: Was he amused to see you doing this?

JD: I think so, yes.

ML: He didn't think you were breaking all the rules?

JD: He probably did, too. He never told me. He's not the sort of person who tells you what he's thinking, but he certainly went along with it. He'd say things like, 'This is unbelievable what you can get so quickly.' I could draw a plate so fast and give it to him. Because you had to wait with Aldo and his people. His people were not zippy. But they were not sluggish, it was that they were so careful.

ML: I am sure that Richard Hamilton told me years ago that when he came to work with Aldo, it was unbelievably expensive because he worked so slowly. It was like a rock band going into the studio and overlaying the tracks. When you are paying by the hour, it's cripplingly expensive.

JD: Of course.

ML: Whereas you would go in like a cyclone, produce something and then get out of there again.

JD: Well, it was unbelievably expensive for Richard, because he was paying for it. He chose to pay for it, after his experience with Paul.

ML: I see.

JD: Whereas I chose not to pay for it. No one offered me. Aldo said, 'I'll pay for it, I'll publish it.' He'd get his percentage, and that was that.

ML: So your speed wasn't from a financial consideration. It was your impatience, as always.

JD: My impatience was tremendous. He drove me crazy! I can't tell you the amount of cigarettes I smoked, waiting for plates. Yet the plates were done precisely, efficiently. These were not slowpokes down there, these were guys who were trained to do it right.

ML: How many people did he have working for him?

JD: He always had one. Michel was the guy. And then he probably had a helper for Michel, sometimes. And then Michel went with Piero, when the split came, and we were glad to see him go. They were perfect together. Just perfect bullshitters. But Michel is a really good printer. Aldo always had good printers.

ML: But it wasn't a whole group of people, it was just one person working with him?

JD: Usually one, or sometimes two. But usually one and a young apprentice. Aldo on weekends would print himself.

ML: But would he always do the first proof?

JD: Not always, no. He'd take it down and have it proofed. But a lot of times, I would come on weekends, between going to London or something, and Aldo would work with me on weekends by himself. We'd work together.

ML: Some of the greatest etchers of the past – Rembrandt being the most notable example – delighted in the continuous transformations that could be effected by reworking a plate, printing impressions at each stage and in so doing emphasising the process of making rather than the striving for a finished product. The subtle transitions and brutal reworkings alike are each cherished for their own qualities. You are very rare among living printmakers in having that kind of mindset, since the emphasis in the work of other artists since the 1960s has been so much on the creation of a uniform edition. Few collectors, in any case, would now even think of comparing the subtle differences of separate impressions. People will just say, 'I'll have one of those', and they get what they get.

JD: Correct.

ML: Nor would most print publishers wish buyers even to look at various impressions of the same print. It would drive them crazy if people were coming in and asking to see eight impressions of the same print. You, on the other hand, have often chosen to reuse a plate after editioning, or to publish a small edition of what would be termed a stage proof...

JD: I think it would be called a 'state' proof.

ML: ...before continuing to transform the single or multiple plates on which you are working. *Nancy Outside in July* is probably the most extreme manifestation of this tendency.

JD: No. It was the first manifestation of it. Since then...when you buy a print, you're getting a different print each time.

ML: I meant that you went through 22 variations of that original image. For the first print you used three plates and hand-colouring, but you immediately started adding other plates and indeed subtracting them as well. *Nancy Outside in July II*, for instance, is the simplest in being printed in black only from just the first of the three initial plates. Then you were reworking individual plates, printing them in different coloured inks, sometimes reprinting the same plate on a single sheet so as to sandwich hand-colouring in between the two layers. According to the detailed descriptions in the ULAE book, you ended up with 16 separate plates used in a multitude of combinations, with some of the etchings printed just the once and others passing through the press as many as eight or ten times. How difficult did it become to keep track of these changes, especially given the fact that you made the series over a period of several years?

JD: I never kept track of the changes. I didn't care once it was done.

ML: What I find difficult to understand, since you were doing these on separate visits here…

JD: He always saved state proofs. So when I came, I would always go through what I had done before. I'd see things that I had done.

ML: But you had to produce each edition before you could go on to the next one.

JD: That's correct.

ML: So would you leave Paris and then come back when he had printed the 30 impressions, and then rework the plates then?

JD: Possibly.

ML: Because you wouldn't have had the time to sit around waiting for him to print them all.

JD: Absolutely. I never had the luxury of that.

ML: So you must have been coming and going to Paris a lot in those years.

JD: I think so, yes. That's when he and I really got friendly. Another thing about him is that I'd have my kids here at various times, as teenagers. Matthew would come because he needed a French oboe. Aldo insisted on taking him to Loret, the oboe maker. Aldo would talk with the guy, with Matthew. The guy would respect Aldo because he knew of him as a printer, because the guy was an artisan. And my kids and Aldo were very matey. Jeremy would come on his way to Rome to meet a girlfriend or something, and he'd come to dinner with Aldo and they'd drink a lot of wine. Jeremy was like 20 years old. And Aldo just loves Nicky. When Nick was 16 I gave him a bicycle here. I said, 'You come with me on the Easter holiday, and Aldo and I will build you a bicycle' – not the frame. You can still do that today, anywhere, here or in America or in England: you buy a frame from the maker, your size, and then you put the component parts on. Aldo and I did this. Just this year at Thanksgiving, Nick came with his wife and kids. Aldo is just like a little boy with them. It's like they are all boys together. He enjoys this male thing that they have. Matthew came this summer, once again to get an oboe, and I happened to be here, working on Pinocchio with Woolworth – just for three days from Walla Walla, because I had to get this done, so we could go further. And Matt came – Pep was still in a coma then, just before she died. We took Aldo out to dinner twice. I've never seen anybody male kiss Aldo. Matthew went right up to Aldo and kissed him. It was really sweet, and Aldo appreciated it, too, really appreciated that day. He said to me afterwards, 'What a great guy Matt is.' They spoke about how you make an oboe. I knew this would help Aldo get off the subject of Pep, that he could lose himself for a minute. He wasn't eating at all. It has been our project to keep him eating. Two days before she had the stroke, Diana and I had lunch with her, and all she could talk about was how worried she was about Aldo. He wasn't eating, he was depressed. They were supposed to be coming to dinner, he calls and says, 'I think she's had a stroke, we can't come.' She was never up again. She was comatose for a long time. During that time he never ate. He was drinking, at first, and then he stopped that, too. He would come here. We'd feed him, and finally I got it right, how to do it. He's a kind of anorexic, in a way. You can't give him a lot. I don't know if you noticed last night. I'll feed him first, I'll give him very little and I'll say, 'Is that all right?' He says, 'Fine.' He doesn't want any more. He can only eat a little bit. He'd rather smoke, and that's not helping his appetite. But he looks so much better than he did six months ago, it's amazing. If he'd only get his hearing fixed.

ML: Going back to *Nancy Outside in July*, did Aldo ever despair over what you were putting him through with that series, or did he revel in the challenge as much as you did?

JD: I've never been aware of whether he revelled in the challenge, or his despair with me. He only said 'yes' to me. 'Yes, we'll do that.' 'Yes, we'll do this.' I'd say, 'How do we do this?' and he'd say, 'This is how we'll do it.' So I'd do it, or subvert it, or do something, or not be able to take it in my impatience. Just to get him to do spit-bite, just to get it going, it would take him so long to get the right mixture, to make this, to make that. I'd be going out of my mind waiting, I couldn't wait to get my hand on the brush. I had to wait till he did this just right, let something dry, and then it would be perfect. I don't require that perfection. I stayed around with him because I love him.

ML: Aldo was telling me, when I interviewed him about the use of aquatint, how he encouraged you to apply it with a brush as well. And he was saying how incredibly skilful you were, in controlling exactly how you were putting it on, rather than just aquatinting the whole plate in the box.

JD: Oh, right. I would never do that. He's the one who introduced me to the spit-bite. I found it to be a very subtle medium. It's just that his practice of it was that the acid was very weak, and you had to keep going over it. And that drove me crazy, because I don't want to go over it: I want to put down my mark and see what I did. I could never get him to make the acid stronger.

ML: So it was like putting washes on in a watercolour.

JD: Right.

ML: So you can have layer upon layer and control the gradations.

JD: Right. That was his way. I actually learned a lot about watercolour painting from that technique. This is what I mean. He was so skilled at so many techniques in etching that everything you said to him, he would produce for you.

ML: You would say, 'I want to get this result on this part of the plate', and he would tell you how to get it.

JD: And he had no secrets, he kept no secrets from you.

ML: When you were saying earlier that it was a secretive place, it was just in terms of his private life.

JD: Oh, yeah, his private life.

ML: He was telling me about the method of colour etching that he showed Hockney, which he had devised for Picasso, who had died before he had been able to use it. Using the sugar lift. And he said that Hockney immediately went back to London and taught Maurice Payne how to do it, and he then did it with Maurice. And I said, 'Did that bother you? Do you think you should have patented this method?' And he said, 'No, it doesn't matter.' He seems very generous in that way.

JD: It would never occur to him to keep it. He's a very generous man. He's overly generous with ideas like that. It's like I went to etch with a guy called Niels Borch Jensen in Copenhagen. And I told him I saw some print he had done, and he said, 'That's my secret method.' And then I said, 'What do you mean? Tell me how you did this.' He said, 'Well, I'll show you, and I'll give you the stuff, but I am not going to tell you how I make it.' He never would. Since then, we've pretty much figured it out in New York. But Aldo would never consider that; he'd tell me exactly what it was he'd made there, how you do it.

ML: Clifford Ackley refers in the ULAE book to some of the highly unusual procedures involved in the *Nancy Outside in July* series, and he maintains that sometimes the image was transferred from the first plate to other plates by means of silkscreen or photogravure transfer. I asked Aldo about that, and he said, 'Never.' And he explained that he would simply print another proof, and when the ink was still wet, transfer it onto another plate, and the ink would act as a resist.

JD: Yes.

ML: So he said there was no photogravure and no silkscreen, because he didn't have those processes, and he didn't send anything out. Do you remember doing anything to the plates outside the Crommelynck workshop?

JD: The only thing I remember specifically is one called *Squeezed out on Japanese Paper*, number 23 out of the 25 in the *Nancy Outside in July* series. That is a rubber stamp that I had made in America. I brought it here, and he inked up the rubber stamp and printed it onto a plate, and then the aquatint was applied around it. Therefore it distorted the image. That's a case of applying something to the plate from outside. What did Ackley say?

ML: He said that the first plate was sometimes transferred to another plate by photogravure or screenprinting.

JD: I don't recall that.

ML: Aldo was sure that that wasn't true.

JD: OK. I wonder where Ackley got that idea? It's not something he would make up. He's a careful writer.

ML: I am perplexed by that, because it would have involved sending things out of the workshop, because they didn't have those facilities. The *Eight Little Nudes* you made at Aldo's studio in 1982, also known simply as *Suite of Eight Prints*, are conspicuous in their simplicity, spontaneity and modesty of scale by comparison with the *Nancy Outside in July* prints that immediately preceded them. Each was printed from just two plates, one printed in black for the outline and the other in an ochre or other fleshy colour for the skin tone. Did you choose to make this intimate and erotic series specifically as a kind of holiday from the demands of the large and complex *Nancy Outside* prints?

JD: I can't remember. I can only remember buying the postcards that I worked from. They were nudes.

ML: From what period? New ones?

JD: I think they were new ones. They were kind of lurid, cheesy postcards of nudes. Unless I found them in a junk shop.

ML: Aldo told me that he remembered you buying an erotic magazine...

JD: Maybe that's what it was.

ML: ...at a newsagent's stand, and coming in and ripping the pages out, and drawing from those.

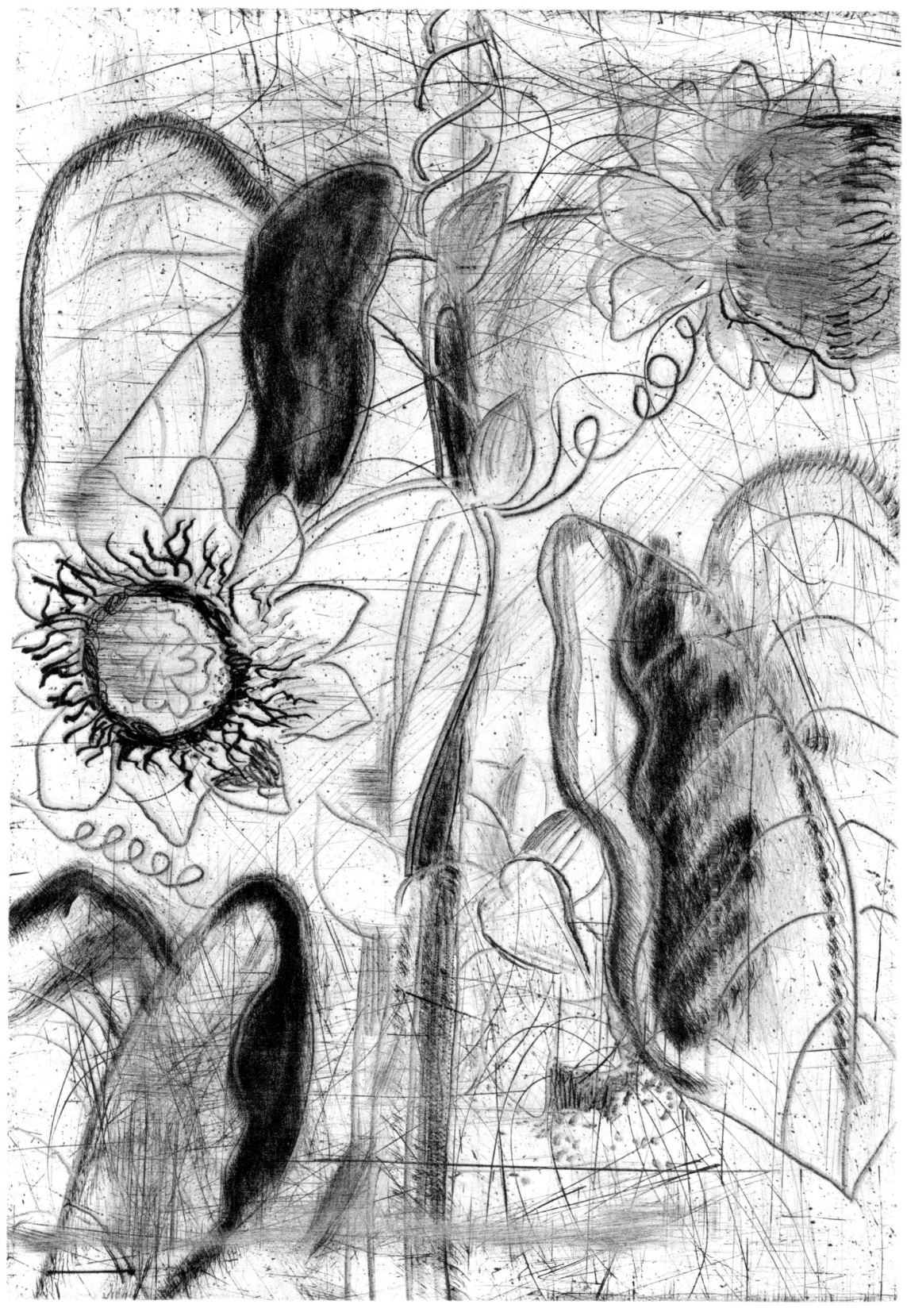

JD: That seems absolutely likely, but I know also that I can see the postcards.

ML: The catalogue note by D'Oench and Feinberg relates these to nude studies by Rodin and charcoal drawings by Matisse, but that wasn't really where they came from. They came from something much more...

JD: Base! Oh, yeah. I just wanted to make some little erotic nudes.

ML: Whatever their artistic antecedents, the images seem to me blatantly contemporary and, well, just blatant: like poses borrowed directly from the pages of sex magazines, which is what they are.

JD: Yes, exactly.

ML: How did you come to reuse three ground-down plates from *Nancy Outside in July* for the 1982 triptych *Desire in Primary Colors*? Were they just lying around, and they gave you a sudden idea of how they might be reused?

JD: Well, as we discussed, I came to Aldo's because I wanted to work, and I said, 'Don't I have some old plates?' Because I had been doing a lot of stuff in other places. I didn't have it in mind that I wanted specific plates. I wanted plates that size that I had worked on.

ML: But it was important to you to have plates that had a history, rather than new plates.

JD: Absolutely, very important. Because I knew that I could get all of that history down and add to it, in very little time. Because I had very little time. I had been working out all this stuff, that way of working. Aldo's place was no kind of place to work out that kind of stuff, you know. I worked it all out on my own, when I had an etching studio in Putney [Vermont], in a little building I had. Or I did in New York or different places, wherever I would go other than Aldo.

ML: I'm jumping ahead again here, but Aldo was telling me about the *Temple of Flora* plates, and he remembers the plates arriving at the studio here, with their polished side and their very rough backs, and he said you just turned them all over and threw them over the floor to scratch them...

JD: Right.

ML: ...just to get some marks. So you could start working on them. He was very amused by that.

JD: It worked out slightly differently than that. I had the plates in London, in my studio at Sydney Close. I drew my drawings and I carved them there, in Sydney Close, all with electric tools. I brought them to Paris, and then I threw them across the floor.

ML: So they weren't virgin plates.

JD: No, I had already worked on them. I scratched them all over, and then he proofed them. Yes, he was very amused by that.

ML: I remember being in your studio, when you had drawings on the floor, and you were walking on them.

JD: Yeah, right.

ML: So you always allow that...

JD: I want that.

ML: ...accident and chance mark, a distressing of the surface.

JD: I love that. As Frank O'Hara said, it's all grist for my mill. I think the more history you get into it, the richer the object will become.

ML: You don't like being precious, even with marks that you might have put a lot of time and trouble into making.

JD: I've always said to Diana, when we talk about drawing, that if you do it once, you can do it again. I believe that. But in recent years I've gotten to the point where I realise that sometimes I can stop, you know, and just keep that one passage.

ML: So I was asking about *Desire in Primary Colors*, whether it was a spontaneous decision prompted by seeing the plates lying around.

JD: I just said, 'Give me three *Nancy Outside in July* plates.'

ML: And it didn't matter to you which ones.

JD: No. I was through with that, anyway.

ML: And a surface like that, pitted with accidental marks, excites you in more ways than a fresh copper plate would.

JD: Correct.

ML: Much of your work with Aldo has been made in serial groups: *Mabel, Nancy Outside in July, Eight Little Nudes, The New French Tools, The Temple of Flora*. But occasionally a single print emerges apparently out of nowhere, as in the case of *Five Shells* in 1982. How would something like that come about? [He asks to look at a reproduction of this print.] In that case it looks unplanned, like something that might have been prompted by a glimpse of the actual objects themselves.

JD: No. That's not how it happened. In the late '70s I was making the *Key West* print, it's a conch shell. I had reproduced it in photo-offset from a drawing with watercolour. I dropped an etching on top of it. At the same time – I spent a couple of winters in Key West [Florida] in the late '70s – I was working on an etching of a shell. I had it on the easel in my living room, on 83rd Street [in Manhattan]. Nancy and I were living there. It was on the easel and I would pass by it and work at it and hope that I could build it up, just by sitting there and doing drypoint on it. Build it up and not lose interest. I had worked on it for months, and I knew it was going to be a good thing, something beautiful. So I called Federal Express – in those days Federal Express had just come in – I sent it to Aldo. I said, 'I'll be there by the time this gets there.' I walked into Aldo's two mornings later, and I said, 'What do you think of the plate?' And he said, 'It never came.' And I said, 'What are you talking about?' He said, 'It's not arrived.' I said, 'Call them up.' He calls French Federal Express and they say, 'Well, the truck was hijacked. We found the truck, but it's completely empty.' We never found the plate again. We couldn't believe this. It was hijacked between Charles de Gaulle and the rue de Grenelle, I guess. And so the plate was gone, and I still wanted to do something. So I started this.

ML: And what were you working from?

JD: A conch shell. I had it with me in my suitcase, because I was bringing it to work on the other one.

ML: So you had to start again from scratch.

JD: Correct.

ML: But you were determined to make a print of a conch sell.

JD: Yes.

ML: The wrought iron gates outside Aldo's house on the rue de Grenelle – the gate through which you passed to enter the studio, and which was in your view when you sat working at the table inside – became a new motif in your art in 1981, subsequently reinterpreted on numerous occasions in prints, drawings, paintings and sculptures. Given that

you conceived of the motif as a celebration of your friendship with Aldo, it seems paradoxical that out of all those variations only two prints using the motif were actually made with him: *Blue Detail from the Crommelynck Gate* 1982 and *Wallpaper in Paris* 1985. It is interesting that when the gate first appeared as a motif in 1981, it was in paintings, and that the first prints made of this subject in 1982, *Blue and Red Gate* and *Blue Crommelynck Gate*, were both lithographs printed at Maurice Sanchez at Derrière L'Etoile Studios. Much to my surprise, when I checked through the catalogue raisonné volumes of your prints, you seem to have produced only one further Crommelynck Gate print – the luscious woodcut with hand painting called *The First Woodcut Gate (The Landscape)* in 1983 – before abandoning it as a subject for prints. Given that you continued to use the gate motif in paintings, drawings and sculptures, it seems almost perverse that you chose not to do so in the prints you made with Aldo, when you had the perfect opportunity to be studying the original again from life. Did you consciously avoid making Gate prints with him?

JD: No. It just wasn't there for me at that time. I had other things I wanted to do with him. And I was printing elsewhere, too.

ML: But you made a lot of other Gates, so I wondered if you felt the need to recall the shapes from far away, rather than observing them at firsthand.

JD: No, I had photographs of them.

ML: But you were still quite free in interpreting those shapes as time went on.

JD: Correct.

ML: You weren't enslaved to those actual gates. It became a more emblematic image.

JD: Exactly. It became another archetype.

ML: The series of five large etchings you made with Aldo in 1983–4 under the title *New French Tools* mark a conscious and deliberate return to imagery that had been at the forefront of your repertoire since the early 1960s, first in paintings and sculptures and later in drawings and prints. They bear particular comparison with three etchings depicting multiple tools that you had made between 1974 and 1976 for Petersburg Press in New York, the most celebrated of which is *Piranesi's 24 Colored Marks*. Surprisingly, given the currency of that imagery in your art, those were the last tool prints you had made, more or less a full decade earlier. Did you think, when you made *The New French Tools*, that it was time to revisit the imagery?

JD: Yes. I probably got to Aldo's. 'What am I going to do?' Or maybe I thought, 'This will make a great series to do with Aldo.'

ML: Did you go out and buy tools, or did you work with what he had in the studio?

JD: I think I bought them. Let me just take another look at the reproductions. Well, not only did I go out, I think some of these are reworked plates from the decade before. Maybe I'm wrong. I guess not. [The catalogue raisonné entries do not suggest such a reworking of old plates, which in any case were of different dimensions.]

ML: Aldo's recollection is that they were mostly tools that he had in the workshop, for putting up shelves or whatever. He remembered you just borrowing things that you wanted to use.

JD: Probably I did, but I probably also went to buy other things. I think both.

ML: They all seem to be depicted actual size. Does that mean that you put them directly on the plates and actually traced their outlines?

JD: Many of them.

ML: The way you did with some of the drawings?

JD: Yes. Actually, *Three Saws from the rue Cler* means that I went round to the rue Cler, which is around the corner, and I bought the saw.

ML: You bought one saw and drew it three times.

JD: Right, yeah, yeah.

ML: *The New French Tools* are notable for the interplay between the precisely rendered shapes of the tools and the texture of the random, almost chaotic, marks and splashes over, under and around them. How did you arrive at those more abstract marks? Was that spit-bite?

JD: Yes, spit-bite behind a lot of the saws, for sure. But a lot of the other stuff is just abrading the surface with electric tools. A lot of that. The little vice I cut down from a bigger plate, and it's called *Wise*, which is my little joke, because Aldo doesn't say 'vice', he pronounces it 'wice'!

ML: When you used electric tools on those, you were very in control, I imagine, you were very experienced by then.

JD: Oh, very.

ML: I mean the marks aren't as random as they would appear.

JD: Correct. But my method is random, and then I stop and look and see what I have done. But they are all related to Aldo and Pep. Number 4, called *Roussillon*, is the name of the café where we always went to have coffee.

And the *Boulevard Victor* [the subtitle of number 5 in the series] is one of the grand boulevards nearby, that I bicycled on.

ML: But when you say they are related, that's in your mind, rather than specifically something that has gone into their making.

JD: Right. I just wanted to title them in a way that related to the Crommelyncks.

ML: There have been occasions when you have etched plates with Aldo and he proofed them, but the edition has then been printed somewhere else by others. The most substantial case of this was with the 29 *Temple of Flora* prints published as a portfolio by the Arion Press in 1984. These were all printed at R. E. Townsend, Inc., in Georgetown, Massachusetts, several thousand miles away from the publisher in San Francisco, so the decision to print in the US clearly was not taken just for geographical reasons.

JD: It was taken for financial reasons, because I had been working with Bob Townsend a lot. I was invited to the Carpenter Center at Harvard and I brought [the printer] Mitchell Friedman, in the late '70s. I made some prints, some self-portrait etchings, and he printed them. Students watched and helped, and we were there for a week. And we also met these two guys who were printers in Boston, through the artist Michael Mazur. Michael introduced us to his printers: one guy was a lithographer and one guy was an etcher. The etcher was Bob Townsend, and he had a great press that he had made. It was a litho offset press with a huge bed, and he turned it into an etching press. It was sensational. He was one of those kind of guys who had a great touch. He could print softly, painterly, in a way. He and I really got on, and he showed me things I could do with mylar, and photo-etch. He would come to Vermont and pick up things, bring proofs. I went to his place [only] a couple of times, because he moved outside Boston. I introduced him to [Arion Press publisher Andrew] Hoyem. I said 'The guy is so reasonable, you ought to use him.' And Hoyem still uses him. And I preferred the way he printed to many things I did with Aldo. It was so soft and painterly. He just had that.

ML: I added up the number of actual prints that had to be printed for that project: there were 29 separate prints in editions of 150, plus another 25 hors commerce. That adds up to 5075 separate prints! Aldo couldn't have done a job that big.

JD: No. The guy's a machine. He's probably not even printing them himself. In fact, I met a girl once in an Italian print workshop in Milan. Alan Cristea and I had flown down there. I met a woman there who was one of the edition printers, and she said, 'Oh, I printed all your editions for Townsend.' I said, 'Really? I thought Townsend was doing them himself.' She said, 'Oh, no, he never touched anything.'

ML: But you were happy with the results? You got what you wanted?

JD: Very happy.

ML: Presumably for an edition of 150 the plates have to be steel-faced after proofing.

JD: Of course.

ML: Is there a very noticeable difference between the proofs printed by Aldo, in the quality of the line, and the ones that were printed for the actual edition?

JD: No.

ML: Because steel-facing is so subtle?

JD: So subtle. And I forget who it was who faced it. I don't know if it was Aldo's guy or Bob himself. Bob did a great job with it. Aldo was the best I had ever seen, until everybody got the hang of it. Aldo had some kind of great steel-facer.

ML: Can you explain how it's done?

JD: It's the same way chrome is put on a bumper. The steel jumps onto the plate: you create an electric current, and the steel completes it. It's quite dangerous, because of the acid that's used. We do it at Pace all the time now. It's done like that [snapping his fingers].

ML: All but five of the *Temple of Flora* prints are derived from Dr Thornton's 1807 publication of the same name, so I presume that you either had a copy of that at your side and just worked your way through them...

JD: I had photographs of my copy. I didn't want to fuck up my copy.

ML: So you had all the pages you wanted to refer to photographed.

JD: Correct.

ML: And then you made quite free interpretations of those images.

JD: Yeah.

ML: There were 31 coloured engraved plates in that original publication, by a number of different engravers after various painters. Why didn't you simply use them all? Why did you make a selection of those and then add a few more from other sources?

JD: I don't remember doing that.

ML: There are 29 prints in your series. There were 31 in the original Dr Thornton. You left seven out and then added five from somewhere else.

JD: Oh, really? It's just me. [Laughs.]

ML: In 1978 you had already produced a set of nine etchings, in quite small editions, under the collective title *A Temple of Flora*, on that occasion working with Mitchell Friedman in New York. So how, then, did you come to make the much more ambitious set six years later? Did you propose the idea to Andrew Hoyem at Arion Press?

JD: I think so. I think I proposed the idea, and then he proposed the idea of matching them with different poets, so he brought in all these poets he knew. We gave each poet their print that they had written a poem for.

ML: The 1978 prints were formulated a year earlier as mylar drawings, which were then transferred to the plates by the method of photogravure; after printing in black, each impression was handcoloured in watercolour. The 1984 prints, by contrast, were all worked directly on the plates, with a variety of conventional tools and power tools but no acid, and were then printed in black inks with no handcolouring. Would you agree that the earlier set is closer to Dr Thornton in its use of colour and decorative opulence, while the 1984 publication follows Dr Thornton much more faithfully in its book format, in its extensiveness and in its richness of intaglio methods? Would that be a fair way of distinguishing the two series?

JD: The first series was more like drawing. The second was more like drawing with a magic marker. I put them all on with a magic marker onto the plate, and faithfully tried to follow those magic marker lines, so I got something with a different look to it. It was more austere.

ML: Did the magic marker act as a kind of resist, or just as a guideline?

JD: It was just my guideline. It can resist over a ground, it can be a stop-out.

ML: But it wasn't.

JD: No.

ML: Were the *First Version* and *Second Version of Hiroshima Clock* 1984 made during the same visit to the Atelier Crommelynck as the last of the *Temple of Flora* prints and *The Philadelphia Heart*?

JD: I have no idea. The *Hiroshima Clock* was made for Richard [Hamilton] for the women of Greenham Common.

ML: The first Hiroshima print was made for that Greenham Common Portfolio, to benefit the group protesting against the presence of nuclear weapons on British soil, but the image also relates closely to the mural-sized painting you made in the same year, *Lessons in Nuclear Peace*, for the library of the Louisiana Museum in Humlebaek, Denmark.

JD: Yes. But it wasn't a mural-sized painting. It was a series of about 25 panels.

ML: I meant as a whole.

JD: As a totality, yes.

ML: But which came first, these prints or that multi-panel painting?

JD: The multi-panel painting.

ML: So when Richard asked for something for the portfolio, you immediately thought that that was an appropriate image.

JD: Yeah, exactly.

ML: You conspicuously avoided using your trademark heart and robe motifs at Aldo's studio until 1981, when you made *A Heart on the Rue de Grenelle* and the diptych *Two Tomatoes*, both of which contained hand

painting for particularly luscious effect. This was followed by the triptych that we spoke about, *Desire in Primary Colors*, in 1982, which includes a robe, a tree and a heart. In 1984 you made *The Philadelphia Heart* there, followed by three prints published in 1985 which came out of the October 1984 session at the Atelier Crommelynck: *Two Hearts for the Moment*, *The Robe in France* and *Red Robe in France*. The latter three are unusual in having started life as offset lithographic reproductions of paintings printed in four colours, then over-painted in acrylic before finally being over-printed under Aldo's supervision from plates etched with soft-ground and worked with electric tools. What gave you the idea on this occasion of combining three distinct processes in such an unconventional way? Aldo had a recollection that those offset lithographic reproductions of the robes were made as posters for something, and that you printed them and then weren't happy with them and wanted them to be reworked.

JD: That's my recollection, too. They started life as reproductions for something else, and they were too dark or whatever. I saw it as another way to make an etching.

ML: As another ground on which to print.

JD: Yes. But they were printed, I believe, in permanent colours by a good printer.

ML: So how much survives of that offset litho under the etching? How much do you still see of it in the final print?

JD: You see some colour.

ML: So there's a residue.

JD: Yes.

ML: Do you remember how Aldo reacted to the suggestion of doing that, which pushed him into a *de facto* collaboration with another printer using a different process?

JD: I promise you, he never reacts.

ML: Those were commercially produced four-colour prints, done photographically.

JD: Yes, but you know, by that time I was his man. He would let me do anything.

ML: *Tools and Dreams* 1985 provides another instance of plates you had made earlier with Aldo – in this case a pair from the *New French Tools* series – being reworked and totally transformed. Did you on that occasion go into the workshop with such a plan in mind? Or would a print like this emerge spontaneously from seeing the plates there?

JD: It could. A little of both, probably, but I think I had the idea. I get a lot of ideas at night. This was probably a marginal thought, that I could use them. I never like to waste anything. The idea of cancelling a plate is absolutely foreign to me, I would never want to do that.

ML: Aldo learned pretty quickly not to cancel yours, knowing that you might want to come back, even years later, and reuse them.

JD: Exactly. The idea that he is sitting over there with all my plates and he has sold his press is so stupid. He could be printing, but he doesn't want to. It's very odd.

ML: When we met the other day on the first occasion, for a drink, and he was talking about Pep, I said, 'It's a pity you're not able to do any printing now, because it would take your mind off things.' And he said, 'Yes, but I sold everything. I can't work any more.' That seemed very sad.

JD: But he's the one who sold it. Why did he sell it? I just don't get it. I understand him

retiring from America. But he could always bring in printers.

ML: Another group of three prints published by Pace in 1985 from your recent session at Crommelynck's have an extraordinary velvety blackness, almost like mezzotints, out of which the white highlights emerge: the triptych *The Channel, My Heart, A Hand*, followed by a single skull image called *The Channel*, which you then cut down, partly effaced and superimposed with a portrait of Nancy as *12 Rue Jacob*. I'll just ask you now, before we go further, what the significance of that address is.

JD: That was the address of the apartment we were in. We had taken an apartment to be near Aldo and Pep for that autumn, in November. We were there for at least a month in that apartment. I did a lot of the hand-colouring for *Lost Shells* there.

ML: He would deliver all the impressions, and you would just work on them in the solitude of your own apartment.

JD: Correct.

ML: These three very black etchings are incredibly rich, luminous, brooding, mysterious prints for which it is difficult to think of a precedent in your work. Did it strike you like that?

JD: I think I was just progressing as an etcher, just being able to express myself clearer, easier.

ML: I have an impression of that triptych at home, and I know some people find it alarming, almost too frightening to look at: like a bad omen. I know you maintain that the skull is not an image of death for you, but even the ghostly remains of the skull in *12 Rue Jacob* convey a sense of mortality, like an ectoplasmic substance leaking out of the head, the spirit leaving the body. Was that intentional, or was it more the by-product of the processes of coaxing a second life out of a plate?

JD: Well, coaxing a second life out of the plate. The first plate has a skull, and if you put another person's head on top of that, you're going to have some of what you're talking about. But also, in retrospect – it's always hindsight – I realise that I knew things that I wasn't telling myself.

ML: About your relationship with Nancy?

JD: Yes, and about her illness.

ML: These things can be rather subconscious. Those prints were made just before you started Jungian therapy.

JD: No, just in it, I think.

ML: But you told me once that you started that period of therapy as a fiftieth birthday present to yourself, so if those plates were worked on in 1984, you were only 49.

JD: So you're right. Those prints were done when Aldo and Pep, Nancy and I, and Michael and Penny Winton, who were collectors from Minneapolis, had dinner together here [in Paris]. Penny told me about how she and Mike were involved with a channel, and I didn't know what a channel was, and she explained the whole thing to me. That's when they were done. That was the year before I started Jungian therapy.

ML: You never met this channel?

JD: No. And they never met the channel, either, they did it on the telephone.

ML: The Venus de Milo became a prime subject of your work in 1983, appearing first in sculptures and very soon afterwards in paintings, drawings and prints. The first such prints, in 1983 and 1984, were woodcuts, lithographs and screenprints. The four Venus prints editioned at Atelier Crommelynck in 1985, culminating in the majestic *Black and White Cubist Venus*, were the first manifestations of the Venus motif in etching. Did it make any difference to you that the original classical Greek sculpture was just down the road…

JD: That it was in the Louvre? No. It certainly didn't. How ironic, you mean?

ML: No, just that it was there.

JD: I doubt it. I was more interested in making these prints with him. I felt it was like the First World War at that point. We were in the trenches, the etching trenches!

ML: And the motif was by then familiar enough…

JD: Absolutely.

ML: …even though you had by then only been using it for a couple of years. So by this time you were reinventing the Venus through your own work, rather than needing to go and look at the original.

JD: Correct.

ML: The plate used for *Venus at Sea*, the first of the four etchings, was completely reworked for *Night Venus and Sappho* and then again for *The French Watercolor Venus*. Then you moved on to another copper plate of the same dimensions for *Black and White Cubist Venus*. You printed an edition of 30 of the first, 15 of the second, only 8 of the third and finally 50 impressions of the final *Black and White Cubist Venus*. Why the did the numbers vary so much?

JD: Possibly because of the handwork involved, that I got bored with doing it. I think also that I have a certain intuition about how much work is out there of mine. I don't want to kill the golden calf. I don't know if you've noticed, but in Paul's [Cornwall-Jones's] day…

ML: They were much bigger editions.

JD: David and Richard did 75 to 100. But at a certain moment I just pulled back and said, 'Listen, I want to go on printing all my life.'

ML: But Petersburg Press was always too greedy about the edition size.

JD: Always, always.

ML: The *Grimms' Fairy Tales* by Hockney were in an edition of 500; Caulfield's *Laforgue*, also 500. Some of those publications were still around years later, unsold.

JD: The same with *Dorian Gray*. He made three editions.

ML: And now, you make prints with only 14 impressions.

JD: At the most!

ML: You prefer making lots of different prints in small editions.

JD: Yes. Exactly.

ML: When you made the first of the Venus prints with Aldo, *Venus at Sea*, did you already have it in mind to make more Venus prints? Or did you wait until that was editioned, and then decide to carry on? Because you would have had to wait long enough in Paris for the 30 prints and artist's proofs of that work to be printed before you could rework the plate. Did you go away and come back?

JD: I must have gone away and come back, because I had to print the Sappho letters, too, so that we could rubber-stamp them. And that was taking forever. So I must have started the one and then wanted to keep on going. It must have been like that.

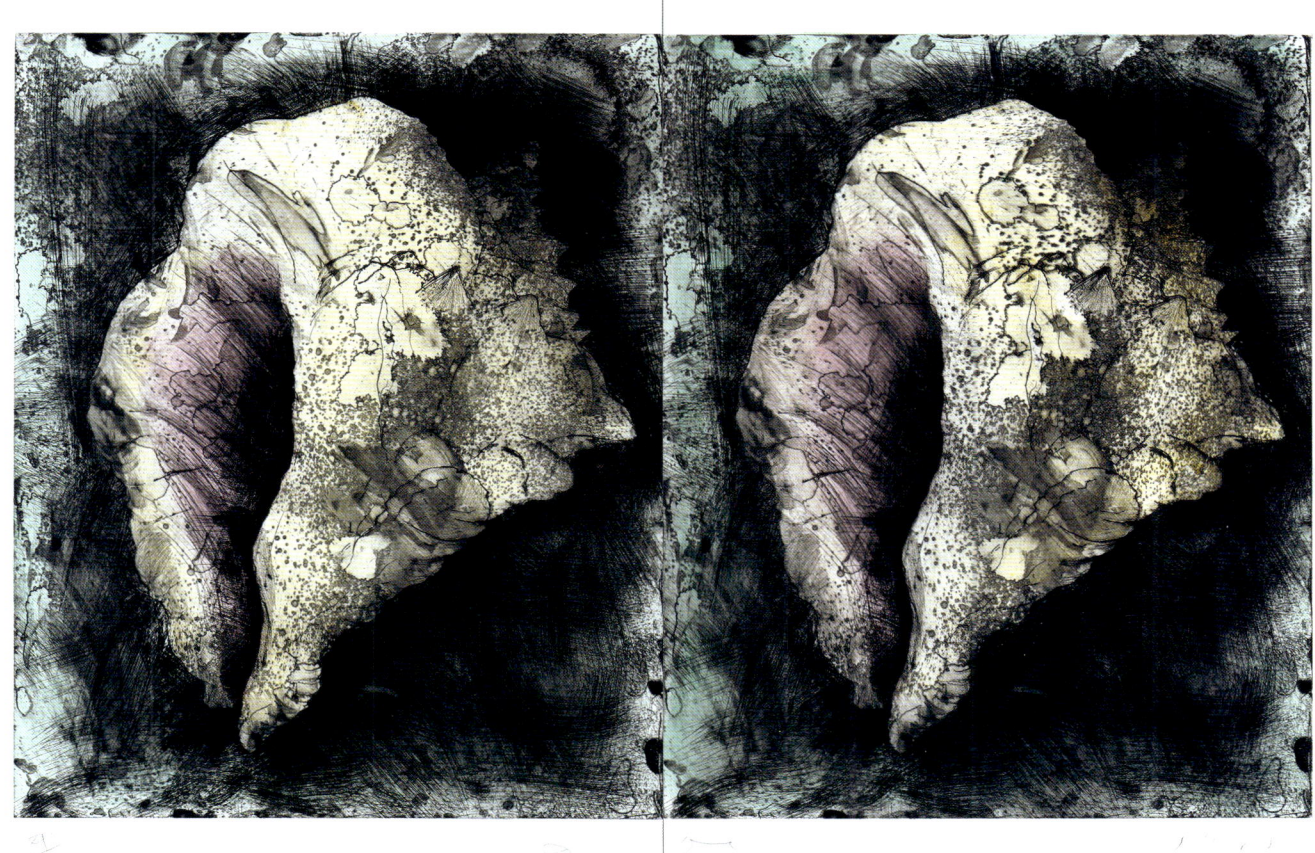

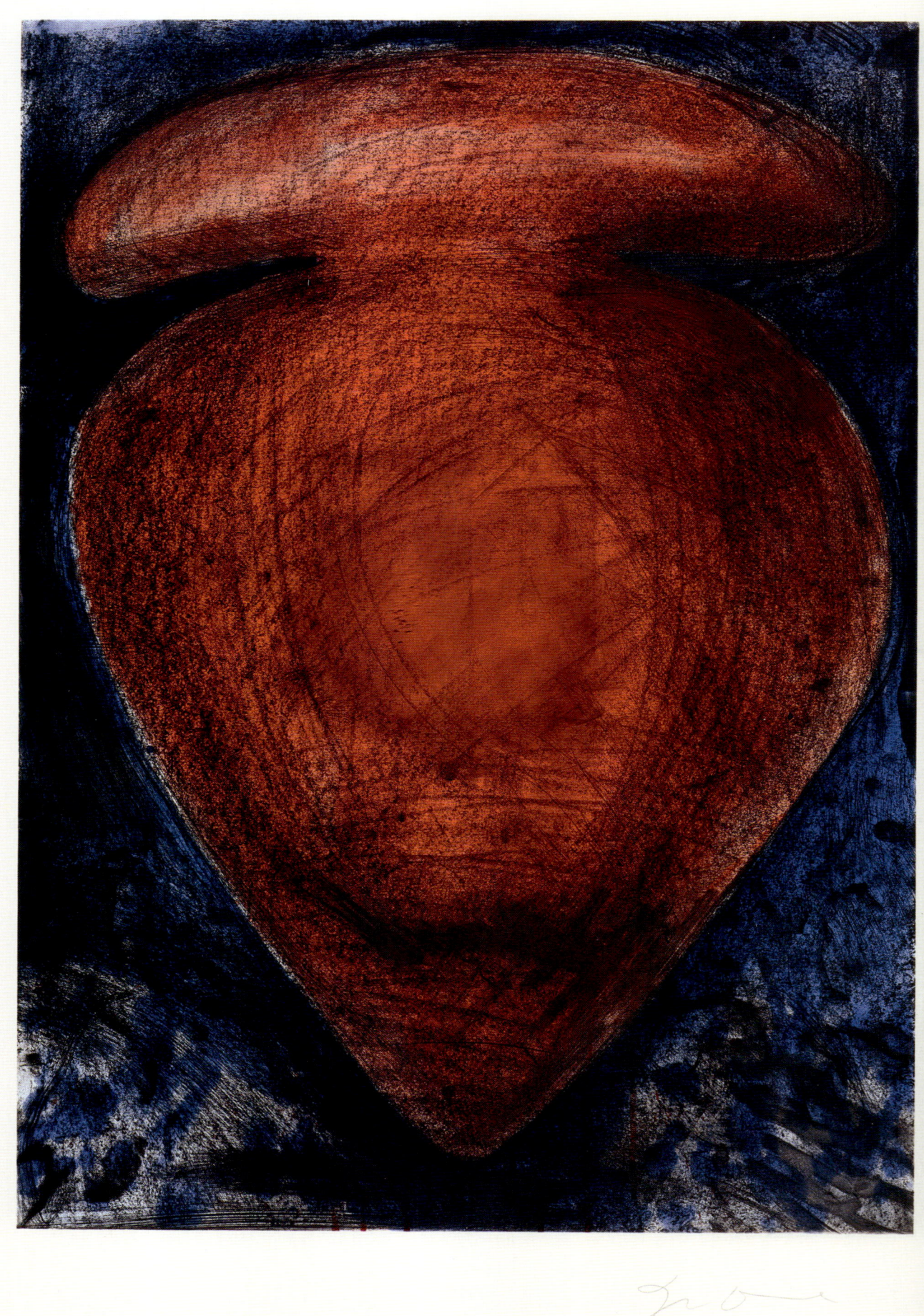

52

PART 2: LONDON, 25 FEBRUARY 2006

MARCO LIVINGSTONE: Are there unpublished prints that you have made that haven't appeared in the volumes of catalogue raisonné, or are even the uneditioned ones there?

JIM DINE: There are uneditioned ones, and there are things not in the catalogue raisonné, but they are few and far between. They were left out by accident: we just forgot about them.

ML: So maybe in the next volume you can do an appendix for the ones you missed out.

JD: Something like that. I am going to have to look into it.

ML: I think it would be a good idea, because eventually there is a going to be a problem with things appearing that haven't been recorded.

JD: There are things that I did with Paul [Cornwall-Jones], when life was ending with Paul.

ML: You were supposed to be doing a series of portraits of London friends.

JD: That was never even begun. I did a little bit and it was not any good, as far as I could get it going.

ML: Was *Quartet* 1986 proofed on the same visit as the Venus prints of 1985, and left until later to be editioned? Or was this a one-off made on a separate visit to Paris? Do you remember the circumstances?

JD: No, other than the fact that the two photo plates were made in America, either by Deli Sacilotto or Bob Townsend.

ML: Aldo said he definitely didn't do the photogravure plates in Paris...

JD: Without a doubt.

ML: But he thought that maybe they had been done in New York.

JD: They were either done in New York, or sent to New York, when Townsend was in Massachusetts. Deli would have been in New York in those years. My memory is that they were all printed in America, and it was not printed in Paris. Maybe it was editioned in Paris, but I think it was proofed on 23rd Street, just before Pace moved to Spring Street. This is my recollection, and that it was the first thing I did with Aldo in America. At that point Aldo didn't allow the printers in New York, at Pace, to edition for him. They were still learning his ways. I really do think the whole thing was made in New York.

ML: What can you tell me about those two paintings that you did the photogravures from?

JD: It was a group of, I think, three or four paintings that [the actor] Joel Gray gave me. He found them somewhere, in some junk store or something.

ML: And why did he think you would like them?

JD: I have no idea why he thought that, but they struck me. They really spoke to me for some reason, and what I did was I stretched them and made a long painting with them which has never been seen. It was in my house for a while. I'm sure I just saw it the

Facing page: detail from *Quartet*, 1986 (see page 58)

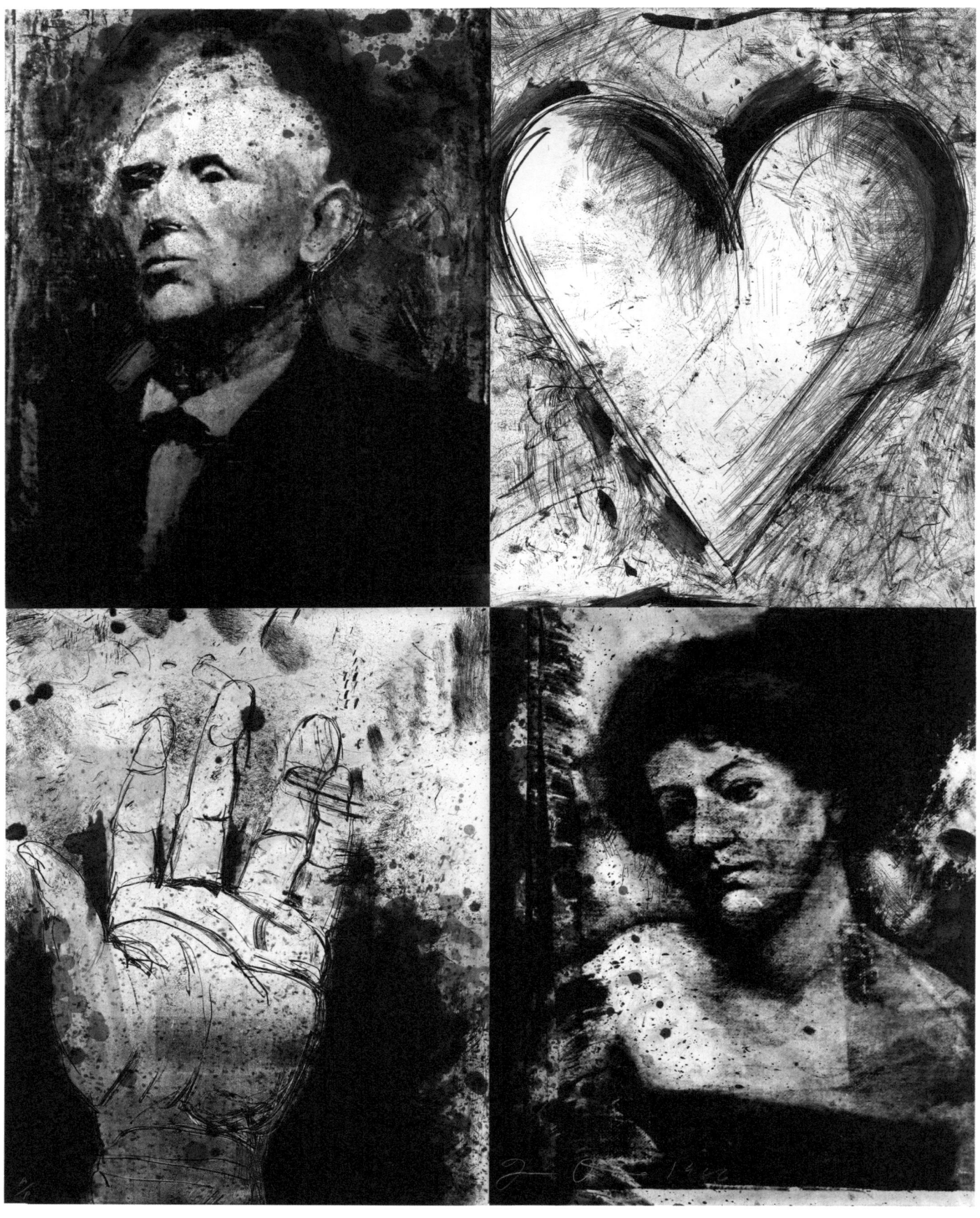

other day in my warehouse. It had other elements in it. It was part of that whole Jungian time for me of using disparate symbols from my unconscious. If it struck me, I used it. That's the sort of attitude I had towards that.

ML: So it was just an intuitive connection…

JD: A connection that I had with things. They were well-painted paintings.

ML: Did you paint over them?

JD: I painted over some of them, yes.

ML: So even though they were well painted, you didn't feel that you had to respect them.

JD: Right. I don't think they were professionally well painted, either. I think they were by some amateur who was well trained. A 19th-century artist, almost definitely American.

ML: Four years were to pass before the editioning at Aldo's workshop of another four prints, two of them bearing imagery that you had only recently introduced into paintings: *Fo Dog in Hell* and the triptych *These Three Dogs are for Nina D.*, both containing extensive hand-colouring.

JD: A huge sense of hand colouring! The one for Nina D. is like a painting.

ML: What did you have for reference when you were making these?

JD: I was drawing Fo dogs at the same time. Also I guess it was part of the Jungian thing.

ML: They appeared in your paintings, too.

JD: Yes, like *Emily Dine, Good News!* They were from, I think, a Christie's catalogue that I had kept for many years, a dog that I had torn out.

ML: So you had never seen the original object?

JD: No. Never. There were about three reproductions that I had, that I had just collected for years.

ML: And Nina is another grandchild?

JD: She is my second oldest granddaughter, after Emily.

ML: Why did you make the connection between the Fo dogs and them? Was there any particular reason?

JD: Not to my knowledge. I was just using them at that time when I wanted to do that.

ML: Why did you feel a particular attraction to the Fo dogs?

JD: They were kind of ferocious-looking monsters, with some sort of nightmarish quality. But they also had beautiful colouring and were very sculptural. I felt I could draw them well, that it would be fun to draw them. And it was. I kept correcting and, as is my wont anyway, I tried to get them to come to life. I was Gepetto again, with 'the talking stick'.

ML: So when you were working on those prints, you had the same reproduction of the porcelain pieces.

JD: Probably.

ML: Rather than reproductions of your drawings or paintings.

JD: Maybe. I don't remember. I remember making the Nina Dine ones at Aldo's, because it was so uncomfortable working there. It was very lavish looking, but in that studio room there was really no wall to pin anything up on. There was only a ledge and a table all the way around, where you could put a plate.

ML: When you were proofing a print, how could you view it?

JD: He had an easel, a drawing board on an easel. It was strange. When he designed the place, he never envisioned that he would be working on such a large scale. They remodelled – when they built the 'Berlin Wall', they closed up the door. They could have put a wall up right there. He could have pinned things to it, but he never thought that way. He was trained another way. He didn't grow up with de Kooning and Kline. He grew up with Picasso making these small prints. I don't think he had ever made a big print. Maybe Matisse is the biggest print he'd ever made. To display the Nina Dine prints, he put up three drawing boards and clips. Clips are the worst. All the great printers use clips, because they don't want to fuck up the paper. They hate me because I am always putting thumb tacks through them. There's a way to get the thumb tack hole out. You iron it from the back, very simple. But Aldo thought that was a desecration, you see. They all do. Tamarind did the same thing. I hate that. But at Tamarind and all these great shops, there are places where artists can see things. You can pin up wall after wall. Aldo's was the most uncomfortable shop you can imagine, although lavish.

ML: One of the other prints editioned in 1990 is a very straightforward portrait of Nancy, the first of her at the Atelier Crommelynck since the *Nancy Outside in July* series came to a close in 1984. It's called *Irish*. Was this rendered from life?

JD: That's my greatest portrait of Nancy in etching. I think it's the most accurate. I think it shows everything. I think it's the best drawing.

ML: Where did you actually work on the plate? At Aldo's? Was she sitting for you there? I assume it was done from life.

JD: It sure looks like it. I don't remember. I know there were state proofs that I liked also, and that I framed. I think there were four, including this one, that I framed together. I think I have that.

ML: How long did it take to do, assuming it was done from life, how many hours?

JD: Not very long. It's very immediate. A lot of it is done with power tools, Dremels and things. The hair. It's very accurate. I'm amazed by it. Nobody ever bought it, either, it's too troubling to have.

ML: When you are actually working on a plate like that, before you have printed the first proofs, how much can you actually see on the plate? How clearly can you see the marks you've made?

JD: You mean, what I'm getting? Depending. Of course, with soft-ground, you always have the pencil drawing, so you see that and you see what you've picked up, so you know what it's going to look like. Hard ground is the hardest to see. Drypoint you can see. I work a little ink in sometimes to see what I'm getting. But you can see. Usually my method is to do it, have the proof pulled and then start to add and erase. By erase, I mean scrape out, burnish, bring back.

ML: With this head of Nancy, the plate measures 21 × 15½ inches. That's bigger than life size, that head.

JD: Oh, yeah. It's a terrific print. And it's just the sort of print that he prints well. He printed it accurately. There was no *retroussage*. It's done richly, but accurately, because there was no need to have anything bucking it up, painterly wise. It was all there.

ML: Most of your portraits of Nancy are pretty severe.

JD: Yeah. Dick Solomon's mother once said to her, 'How can he do this to you?' Nancy laughed it off, but I guess after I left she must have thought, 'Dick Solomon's mother, I should have listened to her!' I was being very, very accurate, I thought. I was putting down what I saw. That's all. And I was a very close observer of her.

ML: But they are not flattering at all.

JD: No, but I never meant them to be ugly. I thought they showed a lot of character.

ML: It's always difficult making a portrait of someone who is that close to you. Everything in a drawing of a loved one can be taken by the sitter as a reflection of how the artist feels about him or her.

JD: I think probably that's what Nancy felt, anyway, but I also think she felt, for sure, that this was a thing for immortality. She knew she couldn't say *too* much!

ML: She was always ready to sit for you.

JD: Always ready. She never said no. In fact, what a draughtsman does is pick on the things that are depictable physically. For instance, if one is getting bags under their eyes...

ML: You exaggerate them.

JD: You could say it was exaggerating, but even that... It's great fun to draw. The challenge is there. Or the eyelid, as you get older, becomes thickened. It makes it really fun to draw, and to see if you can pull that out. Or to sink the eyes back in. This is a romantic idea about drawing.

ML: And about observing.

JD: The romance of observing. I often said to her, 'The privilege I feel being able to sit here and look at you.' It's almost religious, the privilege of doing that, of looking at her. I was obviously, for forty years, taken with her visage. It's one of the few things that held me there, particularly towards the end. I knew her. She was within me. I had taken her in me. She had enchanted me, if you will.

ML: I don't know if I should be saying this, or prying into the situation, but it seemed to me... By the time I got to know you [in the mid-1980s], your marriage was probably already on the way out.

JD: But *I* didn't know it.

ML: Well, I wasn't quite sure what was going on at first, because you seemed to have quite separate lives. But it seemed to me that her identity was as 'Mrs Jim Dine', her whole life.

JD: Yes.

ML: So that's why in every portrait there is an intensity about her involvement as well.

JD: She is a collaborator on these. In many ways, she gave of herself, somehow. Just by saying, 'Yes, I'll sit for you.' But also she gave of herself, like offering up her visage, in a way. And she could be as pissed off with me as she liked, and she would sit calmly for that. So she was a willing collaborator.

ML: And a non-interfering one, by the look of it. She would just let you do what you needed to do without...

JD: She didn't say anything. She might say, 'It's a beautiful drawing.' Or not.

ML: I remember you saying to me a couple of years ago that you don't like drawing other people, maybe people who aren't close to you, from life, because of the interference you get, or people saying it's not an accurate likeness. Having that kind of response bothers you now. So I suppose that's the other privileged thing about drawing someone you are that intimate with, whether it's family or friends…

JD: But this was a special relationship. This was special. I don't know that everybody had this or ever had this. I never saw a drawing of Kitaj's, for instance, where he had that kind of relationship. I'm not saying that his drawings are bad or good, I'm not talking about that. I'm talking about having that relationship. I think Hockney had it at one point with Peter [Schlesinger], I really do.

ML: It's a kind of possession of the person.

JD: And obsession. There's no question that the reason I stayed so long with her was my obsession. Physically, my obsession with her face. It's what attracted me when I first saw her. I saw her the first time in 1954. She was 17 years old and I was 19. It clicked like that with me. So it was a long time unravelling that, so that I could go on into old age without this encumbrance of obsession.

ML: When did you first draw her? Did you draw her in the fifties?

JD: Yes. The first drawing that I have was the day Jeremy came home from the hospital. That was in May of 1959. It's a pencil drawing, rather accurate, three or four days after she had given birth.

ML: *The Foam* 1990, a large double Venus with hand-colouring, and her male counterparts – *Two Dark Robes* 1991, printed on two sheets – were the last Venus and Robe images that you made at Aldo's. I don't suppose you knew, at the time of making them, that you wouldn't be returning to those themes at that particular workshop, in which case it would be misleading to interpret them as elegiac.

JD: Absolutely misleading. I had no idea. I knew this: that I wasn't so interested in working there any more. I had experienced the freedom of other places. The people in New York were getting so good, and so much more up my alley in their willingness to be extensions of my hand. But also their input, the ease of working with them, it was so without stress. With Aldo, it was…

ML: And not having to travel.

JD: I didn't mind that. That's why I kept on printing in Paris and didn't take Aldo up on the offer from Solomon and Aldo to print at Spring Street with him. I printed with other people, because I wanted a reason to go to Paris. I loved the reason to go somewhere to work. That's very important to me.

ML: You like working with different printers and different workshops. Did that ever cause jealousy?

JD: Among other printers?

ML: If Aldo saw that…

JD: He never said a thing. I tried to be discreet. I never tried to flaunt it, with him or anyone else. I never felt jealousy from anybody, and they were glad to have my custom.

ML: It's just that I can imagine it being like any friendship, or like a love affair, that people have a relationship with you and then they see you are going off to see Kurt Zein or whatever, and they might feel that you've found somebody that you like better. It may not even be like that: it's just that they are offering you the possibility of doing something different.

JD: That's exactly what it is. I always went to different workshops because I always got something different. There was a guy, Niels Borch Jensen, in Copenhagen, who was a wonderful printer. I really stopped going because first, A, he cost too much. Famous artists got charged a lot. And B, because he refused to give me a recipe. He was very secretive. We finally got it, at Pace they figured it out. I thought it was very unfriendly. In fact, I would have come more if he had been generous. I thought he made a mistake.

ML: But there are some artists who form a special relationship with one printer, and end up doing everything with that same printer. The danger with that is that it can become repetitive, too much of a formula. They both know what they are doing.

JD: And then the printer takes over – I'm thinking of Maurice [Payne] – and becomes the artist, in a way. A group of prints with an artist ends up looking very uniform.

ML: I was thinking more of artists who have worked with a particular printer over a long period of time. There will be a certain range of procedures, a certain scale, that is possible.

JD: Well, it's like that with Aldo, there are only certain things possible. What was possible was great, but there were some limitations – of scale, certainly.

ML: There are certain workshops like Gemini, or Tyler when he moved to New York state, that became a kind of industry. The kind of printmaking that it favoured was not very suitable for someone like you.

JD: Correct.

ML: Because it was so glossy and mechanical.

JD: Nobody talks about this, but it was really making a reproduction of painting, that was cheaper. So people were getting a big bang for their buck, a big, glossy Rosenquist, that sort of thing.

ML: A lot of it becomes like corporate art: a big scale, impressive technically, but no sense of the hand anywhere. That wasn't what it was about for Tyler. Did you ever work with him?

JD: No. He spoke to me once at Kitaj's. Chris Prater and he came to tea. I had never met him. He said, 'Any time you want to, you're welcome.' I said, 'Thanks a lot,' but I would never have worked with him, and I'll tell you why. It's like Sid Felsen [at Gemini], who I love. I think he's a great guy. When I got to know him in the eighties, Sid would say, 'Any time you want to.' 'No thanks, Sid.' What I really meant was I wanted to print there in the sixties and nobody asked me. I went my own way. The only thing I regret was not being able to work with the lithographer who did the Sam Francis prints. He was a Frenchman called Serge something. I think he had been Dubuffet's printer in France, and they got him to California. The guy was a genius. He was like a painter.

ML: The other print that emerged from that visit to Aldo's studio was *Four Continents* 1991, a huge four-panel etching in a similar format to *Quartet* 1986, but on a much bigger scale. The imagery relates closely to a seven-panel 4-metre wide drawing of 1985, *The Mead of Poetry*, which included images of the Ancient Egyptian King Akhenaton and his wife Nefertiti, and to the woodcuts of the same title published in 1988. This was the only print you made with Aldo using a selection of those particular sculptural heads, though the Fo dog that appears in the lower-left print – curiously, given its derivation, the one labelled 'EUROPE' – had featured in two prints you had made in 1990. What led you to produce this print, which is such a one-off in the context of your work with Aldo?

JD: I did it in 1989 and 1990, I think. I was also making drawings of the same thing. There's a big drawing of *Four Continents* in the show that is travelling now, which I made in Sydney Close in London in those years. I just wanted to do it in print form. And I liked putting unusual imagery for the continent.

ML: Inappropriate imagery, in a way.

JD: Well, the Fo dog that is used in the print that says 'EUROPE', I was thinking of it as my Christie's thing. The stamping was done by Spring Street in New York, with Ruth Lingen, after the edition was printed.

ML: So how much does that vary from impression to impression?

JD: The stamping? It's pretty even. It varies just enough.

ML: Where were the stamps made?

JD: In New York.

ML: Who designed the lettering?

JD: Either I did it, or we chose an alphabet and Ruth had it done. I used them. I use them still in etchings. The whole word is on one stamp, and you rock it.

ML: It's treated like a found object.

JD: Exactly.

ML: In your 'Me and Aldo' essay, which I referred to earlier, you credited Aldo with introducing you to certain technical solutions that were to give you greater control as an etcher. You say specifically that he introduced you to ferric chloride for biting the plates, which he explained to you was a corrosive, not an acid (like the nitric acid you had always used before then), and which therefore cut 'straight down' rather than bleeding through the copper wildly. You also spoke of his 'understanding of powdered rosin for the aquatint box' as 'a physical experience', his collection of needles and knives in razor-sharp condition, and his precision in all he does. In an interview with Susie Hennessy published in *Art Journal* in spring 1980, you drew attention to the different strengths of each master printer you had worked with, saying of Aldo that 'he really teaches technique more than anyone else...he has a vast vocabulary of the process.' Can you recall particular plates that you made with him which yielded results, because of his technical expertise and knowledge, that you would have been unlikely to achieve with another printer?

JD: It's difficult to separate what he knew and what I brought to it.

ML: Is there one print that sticks in your mind that you made with Aldo, but that you couldn't have made elsewhere?

JD: I actually think it's two things. I couldn't have made any of these except at Aldo's. By that I mean, I could have made them all elsewhere, but they would have looked slightly different. One of the reasons is that he really controlled his presses, and his presses sucked everything out of the plate. He had his printers wipe it, with just the right amount of ink, so what it sucked out was exactly what he wanted the plate to have. I had no control over that. I could have said, 'You sucked out too much or you didn't', but I was always pleased with the look. But it was definitely an Aldo print. The one that we talked about of Nancy, *Irish*, I could have printed anywhere, and it would have been a warmer print in many ways, but nothing like this.

ML: Where are those plates, does Aldo still have them all?

JD: Uhm, hmm.

ML: It would be such an interesting exercise to get some of those plates and give them to someone else to print without them seeing Aldo's proofs.

JD: That's a very good idea.

ML: And see what another printer would do with the same plate, and how much actually came from the printer as well as from what is on the plate. The interpretation that he made of it.

JD: That's a great idea. I'm going to do it, I'm absolutely going to do it! That's brilliant.

ML: That would be a way of seeing very starkly what each printer's hand and sensibility bring to it.

JD: Uhm, hmm. The other thing I could think of in answer to that question is the use of sugar lift. I didn't use it much, and I certainly didn't use it with the skill that Richard [Hamilton] or David [Hockney] used. But I never saw anybody else make a sugar lift like this. It worked every time.

ML: I remember you telling me years ago that, when you first visited Aldo's studio, he showed you a variety of tools and suggested how they could be used. Although you were already a very accomplished etcher, you seem to have enjoyed this aspect of tuition, putting yourself again in the position of a student eager to learn all the possibilities of the medium. Do you recall that atmosphere and exchange of ideas?

JD: Oh, sure. But that was the atmosphere in the beginning every time I went. There was always something new to see. Just the way he kept certain pencils for me, or had them for Hockney or for Johns. It was a whole other approach. He was the chef, and in some ways we were bringing the food for him.

ML: But also, you're very open and you like trying different things, and the variety of result that these can bring.

JD: I trust that through chance one meets people and then one gets a suggestion. He and I would talk about places to buy tools in Paris, or he would go to special places just to get a certain kind of bolt or things like that. I went with him many times in his car, and we would go to some dark French little home-made factory, and there would be somebody making some little thing that he needed. I loved all that. And then he introduced me to the basement of the BHV, which is the greatest hardware store in the world, just about. But there was also a wonderful hardware department in the Bon Marché in those years. So through his interest in these sorts of things, I was able to come back and find new products that I had never heard of, or German products like Wolf, I think – a kind of Dremel system that had more possibilities, I thought, for abrading.

ML: The thing is, there are many artists who if they are making something new, would be concerned that it tallies with what they've made before. They want a certain continuity or to see their signature methods. You have that through your imagery, in a way, so when you go back to make a new tool print or something, there's that continuity and that reference back, but you don't seem ever to be very concerned about replicating a nice effect that you got in a print twenty years earlier. You are always looking forward.

JD: I never would go back. I wouldn't remember how I got it, and I just wouldn't want that. I want 'now'. I am a man of sensation. I want this sensation now, to see how it plays out.

ML: I think that's one of the things that made you so open to working with *any* printer, not just with Aldo: that it never seemed to concern you that this might be taking you in a different direction. Actually, you preferred that, to produce something that you couldn't have produced twenty years earlier.

JD: Exactly. And that's what keeps it fresh for me. That's what keeps this, if you will, flame alive. It's one of the ways to keep it alive, by having a new experience like that.

ML: So often now, certainly since the 1950s, a lot of artists make their reputations very early, very quickly – Jasper Johns is the obvious example, at a very early age suddenly appearing out of nowhere and very quickly becoming a world-famous artist – and then the world wants that again and again and again. It's a trap that a lot of artists have to deal with. You've had those expectations, too. Like when the Guggenheim Museum in New York gave you a big show a few years ago, instead of it being a full retrospective it was just the sixties' work again. That's something that a lot of artists have to contend with. The thing that has happened in your prints, it seems to me – although you were always excited by printmaking – is that the prints that you made in the sixties are not the greatest prints. Whereas with a lot of other artists, the greatest work is at the beginning, and then everything else is a repetition or echo or falling off of inspiration. But because you are so excited by the process, the prints get richer and richer all the time.

JD: But also because I draw better than I did, and I am more confident and I am freer.

ML: That process of drawing from life to which you returned in the early to mid-1970s produced a lot of changes in the prints.

JD: Not only that. I'm so much freer these days, drawing on these lithographs I've been making, than I ever was. I just have let myself go, saying 'Can I get this, can I get that? Let's just try it.' But what you talked about also I am experiencing again right now, about everyone wanting Hearts and Robes. It's very lucky for me, because you could say, 'Oh, no, not another.' A, I enjoy painting them. I hope I find something new each time. But also, it affords me to be able to paint other things that I want to paint that nobody seems to care about, or my photographs. It finances that. So I'm lucky.

ML: The very first interview I did with you, in July 1986, was about your printmaking. You spoke in that conversation about the fact that 'It's different [working] with every printer', and you gave special credit to Aldo's input: 'With Crommelynck I get precision and expertise and centuries of French craftsmanship. With other people I get machines or sloppiness or inaccuracies, all of which are grist to the mill. I can't stand printers who think they're artists and who clash with artists. It's a problem especially in America, where many printers are failed artists and they take it out on you.' Do you still feel that way, with another 20 years' experience behind you?

JD: Without a doubt. What I feel is that Aldo was the benchmark for printing. I got prints from other printers that Aldo couldn't have done, but to have known him has been such a privilege, because he informs so many things about me. For instance, he informs the way I cook, because he once said, 'Pep and I buy only the best ingredients,' and I had never thought of that. It's not that I *didn't* buy the best ingredients, I never thought of it that way. To begin with, a great ingredient. No money was spared on that. It showed in the printing. Nothing was skimped, he never skimped on anything in terms of the quality of the aquatint. The quality of everything. I learned that from him. Whereas a lot of other printers did [skimp], and from that I got some good stuff still. And, yes, I do feel that it's an advantage not to be an artist if you're a printer. It's an advantage for the artist who is working

ML: with you, but also for yourself. Otherwise you eat yourself up a lot. That's why the advantage of working with Michael Woolworth, besides being a great guy, he never was an artist. He was always a printer. The same with Aldo.

ML: So there's no ego.

JD: Not at all. In fact, they're thrilled with your result, if it's a good result.

ML: I wonder to what extent all your printmaking activity has fed back into your drawing, particularly. Are there things that you discovered when making prints that went into the drawings that you wouldn't have had otherwise?

JD: Sure. Well, I might have discovered it, but it would have taken me longer. The sense of erasing, and the chance of using power tools on paper also comes from using it on copper.

ML: You used them on plates first before you used them on paper.

JD: Yes, I think so. And I use it now on canvas and on paper... But the idea of using an automobile grinder: when you use it, it can get away from you and keep on drawing without your hand. That is, it would move across the surface following your directions somehow. I have a drawing that's in the show that I'm having at PaceWildenstein in March. It's a big drawing that was up on the wall in Walla Walla for a year. And then I came back and turned on my automobile grinder. I wanted to take something out, and I didn't have full control of it. It's quite dangerous, it can come back and get *you* and abrade your skin. But it kept going across the paper, and it made this gorgeous white puff of smoke. That only comes from my sureness and my assuredness that I won't be let down, because of my experience in printing.

ML: But I suppose you also have to be prepared for the possibility that you are sacrificing something great.

JD: Without a doubt. That's the beauty. It's really fun, and it's dangerous in a way. You sacrifice something and sometimes it goes too far, and then you have to patch it, or you've lost it totally, or in printing, when I wanted to erase and I get more black than I want. Then you've got to go back and see if you can find the disc that will take it down to white again. It's difficult.

ML: When you draw, there is often a sense of the process dictating what happens next: adding another sheet to extend a drawing, for example.

JD: Right.

ML: That's not something I've noticed happening in the prints. I suppose there are cases where you have cut down a plate and made another print from it or something, but it doesn't offer you quite that same flexibility as you have when drawing.

JD: Not as flexible, but I have done it, and I did it recently in New York: adding another plate to the side of it.

ML: I suppose where you give yourself more flexibility with prints is in the hand colouring.

JD: Yes, exactly. And there is more hand colouring than ever.

ML: I interviewed you at length on 1 and 2 December 1995 about many aspects of your work, in preparation for the monograph *The Alchemy of Images*. One of the things we touched on was the collaborative aspect of printmaking. You had just been working with Aldo in Paris, presumably on the prints published in 1996: *A Beautiful Heart, Ex Voto,*

Technicolor and *Technicolor II*, *Owl* and perhaps on *Black Skull* (which was published in 1997) as well. I will quote you back to yourself now, because I would like you to expand on how your work with Aldo changed over the years because of your increasing openness to his suggestions:

> 'I'm a perfect collaborator [...] because I'm able to sublimate myself and take on these other ideas. I just spent a week with Crommelynck, where I thought to myself, "Forty years of etching, I don't know a bloody thing." Instead of trying to subvert him in his techniques, I've taken to listening to what he says. I'm old enough to do that now. Because there's no point to it...you don't get anywhere any other way. I've taken a more eastern, philosophical tack with him, that is, to be passive. Allow *him* to inform me. [...] Just how you put down an acid wash on his aquatint ground. To me it's so exciting. [...He] just says that to me, "You know, you need a little more acid." He can see that, he's just got the feeling, got the feeling in his eyes. That excites me. To stand there with somebody who's caring about that. You get a great image out of him. He's a great midwife.'

JD: That's good. I would say I don't know how to elaborate on that. I feel exactly that way, and that I came to that at the end of our life together. He was then going to retire.

ML: I asked Aldo the same thing, about you saying that you had initially tried to subvert him, and he said that he never took it that way. He never saw it as a battle of wills. The way he talked about it, he was presenting you with various possibilities but it was he who was being very passive and going along with whatever you wanted.

JD: I'm sure that's possible, too. It's always in the eye of the beholder. It seemed like a battle. Not a bad battle, not a bad thing, but a kind of fun thing to do.

ML: He said he was never shocked by anything that you wanted to do, he was amused. 'Amused' was a term that he used a few times in the interview. To see you doing something very unconventional, using electric tools, seeing you make a mess in the workshop! You going in like a bull in a china shop was fine, because you were confident and you wanted to try things, and nothing frightened you.

JD: Also, we had rapport about other things, about life. And his wife was my friend. We saw each other, we had gossip. He knew my kids.

ML: But when you were working in the studio, you weren't chatting away.

JD: A lot of times. Oh sure. And, as I say, he was a great friend to my kids, and my kids love him to this day. They're old men now, but they love him.

ML: It seems strange in retrospect that these turned out to be the last prints you made with Aldo. With the exception of the celebratory Valentine's heart called *A Beautiful Heart*, they are all of rather dark and brooding imagery: skulls, the raven and the owl and a pair of 'anatomical' human hearts, a motif you had just introduced into such paintings of 1995–6 as *Virginia and the Heart*. This was generally a dark time in both your art and your life, when you were separating from Nancy, I guess, and living alone in Berlin. Does that account for the sombre, almost sorrowful, tone of these works?

JD: I would say. And also, I was discovering photography, and some of the imagery came from photographing the taxidermied ravens that I had to paint from. And Germany is dark in the winter, and Berlin is dark, and I was feeling very, very... The Holocaust was with me. You cannot be in Berlin in the wintertime, particularly before they modernised the city so much – it was just beginning, they were digging, it was like a bomb site – plus that, it was a very sad time for me with my marriage. I knew it was over.

ML: But you had already started with your own photography then?

JD: Yes. I started in '94.

ML: I thought you had started...

JD: What?

ML: Again, I think I am being impertinent here, but I thought you started photography because of Diana [Michener, an extraordinary artist photographer in her own right, now his second wife].

JD: Correct.

ML: So you were already seeing Diana?

JD: Of course.

ML: And seeing the photographs you were producing, with their deep blacks, also affected the prints you were making? Is that what you are saying?

JD: Oh, yes, I do. Because Aldo was the first person to print the photographs, the gravures.

ML: But in this case he didn't make the plates.

JD: He didn't make the plates. He just printed them. He had special ink – he got it from the Swiss Mint, and then in New York we reproduced the ink, almost exactly. He printed beautiful copies of these. The first group of heliogravures, he printed them in '96, I think.

ML: So those were probably the last things he printed for you.

JD: Yeah.

ML: That's a strange way to have ended...

JD: Yes, it is.

ML: ...after all the platemaking years, for him just to have printed from somebody else's plates.

JD: Yes, but I didn't know it was ending that way. I didn't know he was going to retire. It's the stupidest thing he's ever done, as far as I'm concerned. Absolutely stupid. There's no reason for it. The man could have gone on until he was dead, with the kinds of gifts he had. He didn't have to physically exert himself. All he had to do was direct people. But instead, he sells his presses from out from under me. I would have bought the presses. And he has all this knowledge, which never comes up now. But you do what you have to do.

ML: He obviously must have felt that he didn't want to be obliged to continue working, and he just wanted time for himself.

JD: I guess. I don't know. Maybe he never really liked working with us, anyway. Maybe he was just so shy and painful, that it was a chance for him...

ML: Most people look forward to retiring, but I don't know any real artists who do.

JD: I don't, either.

ML: And Aldo was really like an artist, wasn't he?

JD: Exactly.

ML: So it's surprising.

JD: In Japan he would be a National Treasure.

LIST OF ILLUSTRATIONS

The first set of dimensions for each work refers to the size of the plate,
the second set to the size of the sheet.

PAGE 2
Aldo Crommelynck Now, 2007
8½ × 6⅓ inches (21.7 × 16 cm)
14 × 11 inches (36 × 28 cm)
etching
edition of 100

PAGE 21
Mabel, 1977 (from a portfolio of 12 plates)
9⅛ × 7¼ inches (23.2 × 18.4 cm)
19½ × 15 inches (49.5 × 38.1 cm)
etching with soft-ground
edition of 60

PAGE 22
Nancy Outside in July VIII, 1980
23 × 19½ inches (58.4 × 49.5 cm)
29¾ × 22¼ inches (75.6 × 56.5 cm)
etching, soft-ground etching, drypoint and
electric tools
edition of 14

PAGE 31
The Temple of Flora XXIV
(Quandrangular Passionflower), 1984
18 × 12 inches (30.5 × 45.7cm)
20¼ × 14 inches (51.4 × 35.6 cm)
drypoint, engraving and electric tools
edition of 150

PAGE 34
The New French Tools 3 – For Pep, 1984
23¾ × 19⅔ inches (60.4 × 49.9cm)
42⅓ × 30⅛ inches (107.6 × 76.5 cm)
etching, aquatint, drypoint and electric tools
edition of 50

PAGE 39
The Channel, My Heart,
A Hand, 1986
3 plates, 19¼ × 15½ inches (48.9 × 39.4 cm) each
26⅛ × 47¼ inches (66.4 × 120 cm)
drypoint, aquatint and electric tools
edition of 20

PAGE 41
12 Rue Jacob, 1985
27⅔ × 25⅞ inches (70.2 × 65.7 cm)
42⅛ × 31 inches (107 × 78.7 cm)
soft- and hard-ground, drypoint,
aquatint and electric tools
edition of 20

PAGE 42
Black and White Cubist Venus, 1985
33¾ × 26 inches (85.7 × 66.1 cm)
41¾ × 30¾ inches (106 × 78.1 cm)
drypoint, aquatint and electric tools
edition of 50

PAGE 45
Nancy Outside in July VII, 1980
23 × 19½ inches (58.4 × 49.5 cm)
29¾ × 22¼ (75.6 × 56.5 cm)
etching, soft-ground etching, drypoint,
engraving and electric tools
edition of 25

PAGES 46–47
Desire in Primary Colours, 1982
3 plates, 23½ × 19½ inches (59.7 × 49.5 cm) each
30 × 65 inches (76.2 × 165.1 cm) overall
aquatint and electric tools
edition of 40

PAGE 48
Blue Detail from Crommelynck Gate,
1982
33½ × 23⅛ inches (85.1 × 58.7 cm) each
39¼ × 51 inches (99.7 × 129.6 cm) overall
etching, aquatint and electric tools
with hand painting
edition of 30

PAGE 49
Lost Shells, 1985
2 plates, 22⅔ × 18 inches (57.5 × 45.8 cm) each
30 × 42½ inches (76.2 × 108 cm) overall
etching, soft-ground etching, drypoint and
electric tools with hand painting
edition of 32

PAGE 50
Fo Dog in Hell, 1990
39⅞ × 29¾ inches (101.3 × 75.6 cm)
48 × 32 inches (121.9 × 81.3 cm)
soft-ground etching, aquatint, power-tool
drypoint and handcolouring
edition of 30

PAGE 51
Four Continents, 1992
63¼ × 48 (160.7 × 121.9 cm) overall
66 × 50⅔ inches (167.6 × 128.6 cm) overall
etching, drypoint and mechanical abrasion
edition of 24

PAGES 52–53
Ex Voto, 1996
24½ × 34¼ inches (62.2 × 87 cm) each
40 × 53⅓ inches (101.6 × 135.9 cm) overall
soft-ground etching, aquatint and power-tool
drypoint and abrasion
edition of 30

PAGES 54–55
Technicolor II, 1996
29¼ × 46½ inches (74.3 × 118.1 cm) each
36½ × 52⅛ inches (92.1 × 132.4 cm) overall
aquatint and power-tool drypoint
edition of 30

PAGE 58
Quartet, 1986
4 plates 17¾ × 14 inches (45 × 35.6 cm) each
35½ × 28 inches (90.2 × 71.1 cm) overall
etching, soft-ground etching, aquatint,
photogravure
edition of 50

PAGE 61
Irish, 1990
11⅞ × 8⅞ inches (30.2 × 22.5 cm)
21 × 15½ inches (53.3 × 39.4 cm)
soft-ground etching, drypoint
and power-tool drypoint
edition of 12

PRINTS MADE BY JIM DINE WITH ALDO CROMMELYNCK

The catalogue raisonné references are to all but the first of the following volumes:

Jim Dine: Complete Graphics (Berlin: Galerie Mikro, 1970).
This first catalogue raisonné predates Dine's association with Crommelynck.

Jim Dine Prints: 1970–1977 (New York: Harper and Row, 1977), interview with Dine by Thomas Krens, essay by Riva Castleman, referred to in the following list as roman numeral II.

Jim Dine Prints: 1977–1985 (New York: Harper and Row, 1986), by Ellen G. D'Oench and Jean E. Feinberg, referred to in the following list as roman numeral III.

Jim Dine Prints: 1985–2000 (Minneapolis: Minneapolis Institute of Arts, 2002), by Elizabeth Carpenter, referred to in the following list as roman numeral IV.

* * *

Reference should also be made to *Jim Dine: Aldo et Moi: Estampes gravées et imprimées avec Aldo Crommelynck*. Göttingen: Steidl, with the Bibliothèque nationale de France, 2007

TITLE	CATALOGUE RAISONNÉ
1976	
Paris Smiles	II/218
Paris Smiles in Darkness	II/219
Retroussage Eiffel Tower	II/220
Drypoint Eiffel Tower	II/221
1977	
Mabel [portfolio of 12 etchings]	II/225–236
1978	
Nancy Outside in July I	III/18
Nancy Outside in July II	III/19
Nancy Outside in July III	III/20
Nancy Outside in July IV	III/21
Nancy Outside in July V	III/22
1979	
Nancy Outside in July VI: Flowers of the Holy Land	III/61
Self-portrait Hand Painted in Paris	III/90
1980	
Nancy Outside in July VII	III/68
Nancy Outside in July VIII	III/69
Nancy Outside in July IX: March in Paris	III/70
Nancy Outside in July X: Young and Blue	III/71
Nancy Outside in July XI: Red Sweater in Paris	III/72
Nancy Outside in July XIII: Dissolving in Eden	III/94

TITLE	CATALOGUE RAISONNÉ	TITLE	CATALOGUE RAISONNÉ
1981		**1984**	
A Heart on the Rue de Grenelle	III/91	The New French Tools 1 – Wise	III/171
Two Tomatoes	III/92	The New French Tools 2 – Three Saws from the Rue Cler	III/172
Nancy Outside in July XII: Green Leaves	III/93	The New French Tools 3 – For Pep	III/173
Nancy Outside in July XIV: Wrestling with Spirits	III/95	The New French Tools 4 – Roussillon	III/174
Nancy Outside in July XV: Nancy over the Trees	III/96	The New French Tools 5 – Boulevard Victor, Double Sky	III/175
Nancy Outside in July XVI: Japanese Bistre	III/97	The Temple of Flora (frontispiece: Details from Nancy's Garden)	III/177a
Nancy Outside in July XVII: The Reddish One	III/98	The Temple of Flora I (Bird of Paradise)	III/177b
Nancy Outside in July XVIII: Full of Expression	III/99	The Temple of Flora II (Iris)	III/177c
Nancy Outside in July XIX: The Fish in the Wind	III/100	The Temple of Flora III (Chinese Limodorum)	III/177d
Nancy Outside in July XX: Among French Plants	III/101	The Temple of Flora IV (Tulip)	III/177e
Nancy Outside in July XXI: The Red Frame	III/102	The Temple of Flora V (Pontic Rhododendron)	III/177f
Nancy Outside in July XXII: Ten Layers of Gray	III/103	The Temple of Flora VI (Snowdrop)	III/177g
Nancy Outside in July XXIII: Squeezed Out on Japanese Paper	III/104	The Temple of Flora VII (Lady's Slippers)	III/177h
Nancy Outside in July XXIV: Brilliant Dutch Gloss	III/105	The Temple of Flora VIII (Perian Cyclamen)	III/177i
Nancy Outside in July XXV: Charcoal Cyclamen	III/106	The Temple of Flora IX (Superb Lily)	III/177j
		The Temple of Flora X (Yellow Pitcher Plant)	III/177k
1982		The Temple of Flora XI (Carrion Flower)	III/177l
The Heart Called Paris Spring	III/118	The Temple of Flora XII (Auricula)	III/177m
Desire in Primary Colours	III/120	The Temple of Flora XIII (Blue Egyptian Water Lily)	III/177n
Five Shells	III/121	The Temple of Flora XIV (Narrow-Leaved Kalmia)	III/177o
Blue Detail from the Crommelynck Gate	III/122	The Temple of Flora XV (Carnation)	III/177p
Eight Little Nudes [set of 8 etchings]	III/123–130	The Temple of Flora XVI (Dragon Arum)	III/177q
		The Temple of Flora XVII (Shooting Star)	III/177r

TITLE	CATALOGUE RAISONNÉ	TITLE	CATALOGUE RAISONNÉ
The Temple of Flora XVIII (Madonna Lily)	III/177s	**1986**	
		The Channel, My Heart, A Hand	III/188
The Temple of Flora XIX (Daylily)	III/177t	Snow in France	IV/9
The Temple of Flora XX (Hyacinth)	III/177u	Quartet	IV/10
The Temple of Flora XXI (Rose)	III/177v		
The Temple of Flora XXII (Winged Passionflower)	III/177w	**1988**	
		Skull [print included in *Nouvelles de l'estampe*], reproduced in *Aldo et moi*, page 14	
The Temple of Flora XXIII (Blue Passionflower)	III/177x		
The Temple of Flora XXIV (Quadrangular Passionflower)	III/177y	**1990**	
The Temple of Flora XXV (Powder-Puff Tree)	III/177z	Fo Dog in Hell	IV/36
		These Three Dogs are for Nina D	IV/37
The Temple of Flora XXVI (Shell Ginger)	III/177aa	Irish	IV/38
		The Foam	IV/39
The Temple of Flora XXVII (Sacred Lotus of the East)	III/177bb	**1991**	
The Temple of Flora (Details from Nancy's Garden, State 2)	III/177cc	Two Dark Robes	IV/40
		Four Continents	IV/41
The Philadelphia Heart	III/178		
Hiroshima Clock, first version	III/180	**1996**	
Hiroshima Clock, second version	III/181	Technicolor	IV/110
		A Beautiful Heart	IV/111
1985		Ex Voto	IV/112
Two Hearts for the Moment	III/183	Technicolor II	IV/113
The Robe in France	III/184	Owl	IV/114
Red Robe in France	III/185		
Lost Shells	III/186	**1997**	
Wallpaper in Paris	III/187	Black Skull	IV/115
12 Rue Jacob	III/188		
Tools and Dreams	III/191		
The Channel	III/189		
Venus at Sea	III/192		
Night Venus and Sappho	III/193		
The French Watercolour Venus	III/194		
Black and White Cubist Venus	III/195		

Talking about Aldo has been designed by
Peter Willberg and printed in England by Granite.
It is set in Berthold Walbaum
and printed on Inuit High White and Amadeus.

The slipcased *de luxe* edition consists of
seventy-five copies numbered 1/75 to 75/75 and
twenty-five *hors commerce* copies numbered HC I/XXV to XXV/XXV.
With each copy is a signed original etching by Jim Dine
entitled *Aldo Crommelynck Now*, numbered as above and with twenty artist's proofs
numbered AP 1/20 to AP 20/20. The plate was made by Jim Dine at
Pace Editions in New York and at the artist's print studio in Walla Walla, Washington,
with the assistance of Julia D'Amario and Bill Hall.
The etchings were printed on 300gsm Hahnemühle copperplate warm white paper
by Julia D'Amario in New York in December 2007.
The *de luxe* edition has been bound and slipcased by The Fine Book Bindery.

The regular edition, in its first printing,
consists of 900 soft-bound copies.